SAVE LIKE A KEEPER

BEN LYTTLETON

PUFFIN

To ABC, with love

PUFFIN BOOKS

UK | USA | Canada | Ireland | Australia
India | New Zealand | South Africa

Puffin Books is part of the Penguin Random House group of companies
whose addresses can be found at global.penguinrandomhouse.com

www.penguin.co.uk   www.puffin.co.uk   www.ladybird.co.uk

Penguin
Random House
UK

First published 2026
001

Text copyright © Ben Lyttleton, 2026
Illustrations copyright © Dynamo Limited, 2026

The moral right of the author and illustrator has been asserted

Text design by Dynamo Ltd, based on original design by Nigel Baines
Printed in Great Britain by Clays Ltd, Elcograf S.p.A.

The authorized representative in the EEA is Penguin Random House Ireland,
Morrison Chambers, 32 Nassau Street, Dublin D02 YH68

A CIP catalogue record for this book is available from the British Library

ISBN: 978–0–241–76571–5

All correspondence to:
Puffin Books, Penguin Random House Children's
One Embassy Gardens, 8 Viaduct Gardens, London SW11 7BW

CONTENTS

INTRODUCTION

**Imagine you're playing in a World Cup final.
You're the goalkeeper for your national team.
(Congratulations, by the way!)**

All of your family and friends are in the stadium watching you play for your country. Millions more people are watching on television all around the world.

This is the most important match of your life so far.

With less than one minute to go, the score is tied at 3–3. (It's been a **really** exciting game!)

Suddenly, the opposition launches a long pass towards your goal. The ball flies over the head of one of your defenders and bounces into the path of their striker.

The striker has to wait for the ball to drop . . . then they are clean through on goal. They're inside the penalty area and have only one player to beat: you.

What's your next move?

Well, this is where I can help you.

This exact scenario happened to Argentina goalkeeper Emiliano Martínez in the last minute of the 2022 World Cup final. The opponent was France, the striker was Randal Kolo Muani, and the whole world was expecting the ball to cross the goal line, the net to bulge and France to win the World Cup.

Martínez had other ideas.

It took a little over three seconds from the time the ball was launched forward to the moment that Kolo Muani took his shot.

In that time, these thoughts probably went through Martínez's mind:

That's an awful lot of thoughts in a very short amount of time! Let's see what happened . . .

As the ball drops, Kolo Muani shoots. He smashes the ball hard and low. It's on target. Martínez spreads himself like a starfish . . . and blocks the ball with his left instep!

It is an **incredible** save.

The save of the tournament!

Minutes later, Argentina win the World Cup after a penalty shoot-out. (Martínez also helps them win that, as I will explain later.) But it was his last-minute save that made all the difference.

If Kolo Muani had scored in that final minute, France would have won 4–3. But instead, Argentina went on to win the game. And Martínez was the hero.

Most people would agree that goals are the most exciting, most dramatic and most beautiful part of football. Headers, volleys, bangers, bundles, worldies, screamers, flicks, lobs, chips and scuffs. They all count. And after each goal, what happens?

EVERYONE GOES WILD!

Celebrations, back-flips, dances and shirt-waving. Cheers from fans can be heard across the stadium. The goalscorer is treated like a hero. All their teammates crowd around to congratulate, high-five or hug the scorer.

And Martínez? What happened after he made the save that went on to change the entire course of the match? The game just continued. The ball was still on the pitch, and everyone was focusing on the final twenty seconds of play. There was no celebration or congratulations. No high-fives or hugs. And certainly no back-flips! It was straight back to work.

This is one of the toughest parts of being a goalkeeper. You make a game-changing save. You prevent a goal. You could be the difference between your team winning or losing. But you don't get to celebrate!

This bothers Mary Earps, one of England's greatest ever goalkeepers, who helped England win the Euros in 2022 and get to the World Cup final in 2023.

'Goalkeepers deserve to be treated the way you treat strikers,' says Earps. 'A save should be celebrated in the same way as a goal.'

The thing is, goalkeepers have always been a bit different to the rest of the team. They wear a different colour shirt from the other players. They are the only ones allowed to use their hands. There is only ever one of them in the team at a time. And, unlike their teammates, who get the chance to celebrate their achievements on the pitch, they haven't always got the recognition that they deserve.

In fact, in the first game in Europe involving professional teams, where players were first given numbers on their shirts in the 1920s, the numbers started at two and went up to eleven. There was no number one. Goalkeepers were left out. How unfair!

Even now, when we talk about formations and tactics, we often name only ten players on the pitch. For example, the team that plays with one goalkeeper, four defenders, three midfielders and three attackers is described as playing a 4-3-3. Not a 1-4-3-3. There are lots of other formations teams use, such as a 4-2-3-1, or a 3-5-2 or a 4-4-2. None of them include the keeper. Outrageous!

Things are changing, however. Nowadays, the goalkeeper has become one of the most important positions on the pitch. And this is because their role has changed quite a lot over the years.

Of course, the main job of the goalkeeper is still to stop shots from crossing the goal line and becoming goals. But now they are also expected to play like a goalkeeper and an outfield player. We call them goalkeepers, but as we will learn throughout this book, they are also passers, attackers and analysts – that's a lot of jobs for one person. (No wonder goalkeeper is not a position that everyone wants to play in!)

And there's more! The best goalkeepers act like a coach on the pitch, ensuring their teammates are all in the best position. Where the goalkeeper stands on the field gives them a good view of the whole pitch. They can see where opposition players are heading, and can tell their teammates where danger might come from and how to stop it.

And at the same time, they need to be alert and on the lookout for shots, which might come from any distance, at any angle, at any moment.

To do all this, a goalkeeper needs to be **brave**. They need to be **strong** and **determined**. They need **focus** and **resilience**. They need a **loud voice** and **leadership skills**. Of course, it also helps if they can catch and they like diving!

This is what two of the best goalkeepers in the world think about their position:

EDERSON, BRAZIL

'To be a goalkeeper is to be a hero and a villain at the same time. It's intense!'

But beware! With such an important role comes **a lot** of responsibility. Every action the goalkeeper makes has far more risk attached to it.

If a striker makes a mistake and misses a scoring chance, they could get another chance later in the game.

If a midfielder makes a mistake and gives the ball away, they could chase it back and win the ball again.

If a defender makes a mistake and doesn't tackle effectively, the goalkeeper is there to save the day.

But if a goalkeeper, the last line of defence, makes a mistake . . . it usually ends with the other team scoring a goal.

That's where this book comes in! I'm going to teach you all the skills you need to play like a pro goalkeeper.

You will learn how to stand in the right position and the best ways to catch a ball. I will show you drills to help you jump higher, leap further and kick more accurately. You will discover how to cope with mistakes and communicate clearly (with and without words 👍).

MARY EARPS, ENGLAND

'You're not part of the furniture, it's an important position . . . Goalkeeping is cool!'

You will meet some interesting characters along the way, including goalkeepers who:

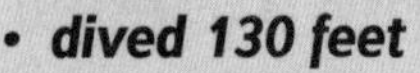

- *dived 130 feet*

- *played in a superhero kit*

- *peed in their own goal*

- *killed a seagull with a goal kick*

- *played with a broken neck*

- *broke their own crossbar*

- *scored more than 100 goals*

- *showered in their goalkeeper gloves*

Plus, Martínez, Earps and many other goalkeeping greats will share their top tips for saving goals and winning matches.

Before you start learning all you need to become a better goalkeeper, I just need to ask you a few questions.

Do you love football?

Do you like having lots of responsibility?

Is your eyesight good enough to read this page?

Can you do an impression of any of your teachers?
(I promise this one will make sense soon.)

If you answered YES to all of these questions, you are ready to SAVE LIKE A KEEPER!

Let's dive in!

PLAYER POSITIONS

When we look at the best ways to save shots, our focus will be on the goalkeeper and occasionally the defenders. All goalkeepers need to consider the movement and positioning of the attacking players they are facing. Here is an example of the formation of how a team may line up.

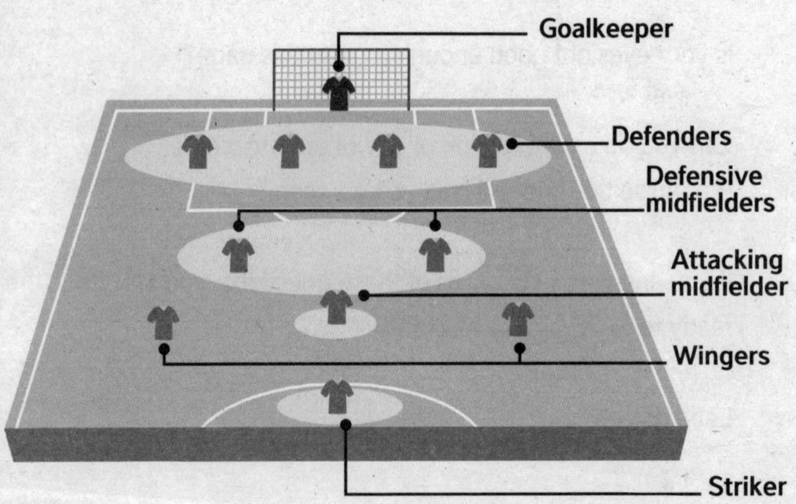

PITCH MARKINGS

The Laws of the Game state that every pitch must be rectangular and, for professional matches, have the following pitch markings. Most goals are scored inside the penalty area, and certain areas of the pitch, like the goal area, the penalty area and the penalty spot, are the same size and distance in every stadium.

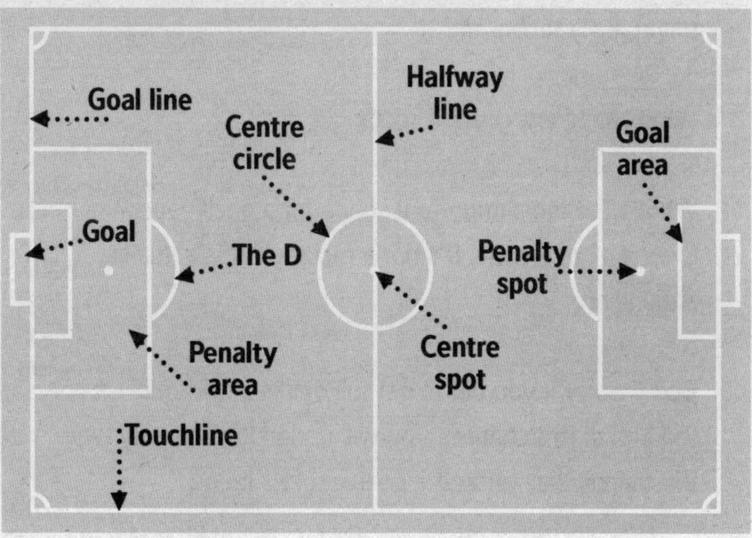

1
POSITIONING

We're going to start this chapter with a geometry quiz.

What shape is a football? A circle (or sphere if you're being really technical)!

What shape is a goal? A rectangle.

What's the most important shape for a goalkeeper? Clue: it's not a circle. It's not a rectangle. It's actually . . . a triangle!

Don't worry if you didn't get full marks in this quiz – by the end of this chapter, you will understand exactly why the triangle has to be the goalkeeper's friend.

During every moment in a game, the goalkeeper needs to be in the right position – even when their team has possession of the ball.

When a goalkeeper is in the right position, they can stop the ball from reaching a player who wants to shoot. They can also catch or block a cross, which is a pass from a wide position into a central position near the goal. However it's done, being in the right position stops potential chances from becoming actual chances!

This chapter will explain the best positions you can be in as the goalkeeper, including:

- How to stand before facing a shot
- Where to stand at certain moments in the game
- How to protect your near post

Just remember: know your triangles! You'll get the point soon!

SET POSITION

We're going to start by considering the most important position on the pitch – yours!

Think of it this way:
you can't throw a party
unless you're ready.

How to throw a party

- Invite people
- Buy a cake
- Party!

How to go on holiday

- Book transport
- Pack swimsuit
- Buy suncream
- Holiday!

You can't go on holiday unless you're ready.

And you can't make a save unless you're ready.
But how should you prepare?

When facing a shot, every goalkeeper needs their body to be in the right position to make the save. We call this the 'set position'. As in: are you ready? Get set!

The set position for all goalkeepers is to stand with knees apart, slightly leaning forward, elbows bent and hands out.

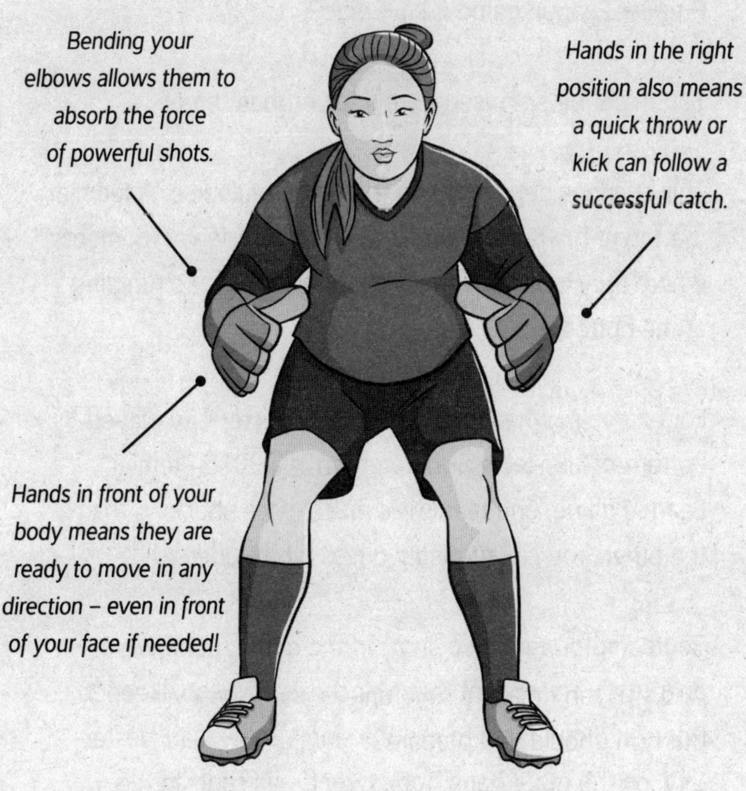

Now you've got yourself **ready**. You are all **set**. You can . . . **go!**

Guess how many saves a goalkeeper makes in a
Premier League game on average?

You might be surprised . . . it's fewer than three!

This changes depending on the team, of course. A team at
the top of the table is likely to experience fewer moments
where they need to defend the goal than one struggling
at the bottom.

For example, when high-flying Manchester City played
bottom-of-the-table Southampton in a 2025 Premier
League game, one team was much more attacking than
the other. You can probably guess which one!

Southampton took two shots in the game (none were
on target). This meant that Manchester City goalkeeper
Ederson didn't need to make a single save. Manchester
City, on the other hand, took twenty-six shots in the
game (only five were on target). So Southampton
goalkeeper Aaron Ramsdale had much more saving to do.
He made four saves in the game, and was named Player
of the Match.

During most of that game, both goalkeepers were waiting and watching. But this didn't mean they could relax. They always needed to be alert and attentive. Maybe it looked like they were standing around and not really part of the action. But that's not true: they were watching everything closely and making sure they were ready when it mattered most.

In fact, the moments of action for a goalkeeper – when they need to make a save – last only a few seconds. Yet they can make all the difference.

So what exactly are goalkeepers doing when they aren't saving goals? There are four stages for goalkeepers during a match.

STAGE ONE: PREPARATION

The goalkeeper reacts to wherever the ball is on the pitch and adjusts their position – especially if the opposition has possession. This stage can last a long time. The goalkeeper always needs to be aware of where the ball is and where it's going next. If the ball is in a wide position (nearer the sides of the pitch rather than the middle of the pitch), for example, the goalkeeper should move closer to that side of the pitch.

Even if the goalkeeper's team has a corner kick, and most of their teammates are at the other end of the pitch, they can never switch off! The opposition goalkeeper might catch the corner and throw the ball to their teammate, who runs quickly towards the goal before the defenders have come back. So being prepared is key!

STAGE TWO: APPROACH

The goalkeeper can see the onrushing opponent is going to shoot, and makes sure they adjust themselves so they are in the best position to save it. That requires getting into the set position before the shot is taken, and reacting as quickly as possible after it.

A shot from distance will give the goalkeeper more time to prepare to make a save than a shot from close range. This is why most teams try to get the ball as close to the goal as possible before shooting. The closer they are, the easier it is to score.

STAGE THREE: ACTION

The moment of the save itself. This stage lasts two seconds at most, and how successful the goalkeeper is in this moment depends on whether the first two stages have gone well. If the keeper has been alert and been following the ball, and has got into the set position early enough, they are far more likely to make the save.

STAGE FOUR: RESET

After the moment of action, the goalkeeper has to reorganize, reset and be ready for whatever comes next – whether it's a corner, a goal kick, or jumping up to stop a rebound.

These four stages work in order. If the preparation stage goes wrong, then the approach and action will be a disaster. For example, the goalkeeper who stays on their goal line when a striker is running towards them, and doesn't adjust their position based on where the striker is, will not be in the best position when the shot is taken. (We will learn more about this on page 28.)

The preparation stage is the most important for all successful goalkeepers. If you can prepare and get the position right, the rest will follow.

Now, let's meet a goalkeeper who has mastered this.

POLE POSITION

Here are two ways to stop your annoying brother from messing up your bedroom.

One: Let him into your bedroom and ask him not to mess it up.
Two: Don't let him into your bedroom.

If the only thing you want to achieve is keeping your bedroom tidy (rather than not upsetting the little squirt!), which option do you think would be more successful?

In option one, you are hoping your brother will listen to you and not mess up your room.

In option two, there's no way he can mess it up, as he's not even in the room.

The same is true for goalkeepers!

The most effective way to protect the goal is to stop the ball from going anywhere near it. Just as your brother can't mess up your bedroom if he's not in it, the ball cannot go in the goal if it's nowhere near it.

This is known as zonal defence. It describes when a goalkeeper defends the zone, or area, around their goal to stop opportunities from becoming shots. Zonal defence only works when the goalkeeper's positioning is perfect. And someone who has mastered this perfect positioning is Spanish goalkeeper David Raya. When he was first called up to the Spain squad in 2022, the headlines across fourteen different newspapers and websites were all the same:

'WHO IS DAVID RAYA?' ¿QUIÉN ES DAVID RAYA?
'WHO IS DAVID RAYA?' ¿QUIÉN ES DAVID RAYA?
'WHO IS DAVID RAYA?' ¿QUIÉN ES DAVID RAYA?
'WHO IS DAVID RAYA?' ¿QUIÉN ES DAVID RAYA?
'WHO IS DAVID RAYA?' ¿QUIÉN ES DAVID RAYA?

If that seems rude (and it was, really), Raya didn't
mind. At the time, he had never played professionally in
Spain, and he'd only played fifteen times in the Premier
League, for Brentford. Before this, he had signed for
Blackburn Rovers aged sixteen, featured for Southport in
the fifth division aged eighteen and moved to Brentford
aged twenty-four.

His goalkeeping coach at Brentford, Iñaki Caña, taught
him how to use his position on the pitch to stop things
from happening before they even happened.

By the time he was spotted by Spain, he was leading the
charts for catches, punches (clearing the ball with your
fist) and challenges won. These are all things that end an
attacking move before a shot comes in.

Raya was proactive, in control and dominated his area.
(And his passing was so good that Liverpool's coach
at the time, Jürgen Klopp, said that he could play as a
number ten, an attacking position usually reserved for
the best passers in a team.) What was Raya's superpower? His positioning.

Instead of just standing on his line, waiting to make a save, he would step forward and rush out to punch or clear the ball before it could turn into a header or shooting opportunity. His average distance from goal for defensive actions (that means how far he was from goal whenever he touched the ball) was over eighteen yards, which puts him on the edge of the penalty area. In 2025, that was the second-highest distance of all goalkeepers in the Premier League!

'People don't notice if there are no saves,' Raya says. 'They don't see that your position prevented it, that you've cut out the ball through or covered an area where a chance might have fallen.'

Not all people, David! Mikel Arteta, the coach who signed him to join Arsenal in 2023, is someone who did notice his clever positioning skills.

'What I like about David is the things he does in goal and the things he prevents that sometimes you don't even see because they don't happen – because he has anticipated them,' Arteta says.

I also noticed, David, as you can see from this chapter!

Raya rates highest in the Premier League for goalkeepers stopping crosses reaching their target. And his sense of positioning is at the heart of his game.

Do you know what else? Raya has a brother called Oscar who encouraged him to be a goalkeeper when he was young. And I don't know this for sure, but I'm guessing Oscar also tried to mess up his bedroom . . . Zonal defence all the way!

Did you know? David is by far the most common first name for goalkeepers in Premier League history. Between 1992 and 2025, ten goalkeepers called David started over 1,600 matches in total in the Premier League. Former England goalkeeper David James (572 games) and Spain goalkeeper David de Gea (415 games) lead the appearances count. The next most common name for Premier League goalkeepers is Mark (over 1,000 games), then Steve (400 games) and Kevin (350 games).

THE RIGHT ANGLE

Look in your pencil case. What have you got? A pencil. A rubber. Maybe a sharpener. These are useful for your lessons at school, but not hugely helpful for becoming a top goalkeeper.

What else have you got? A highlighter. A calculator. Lip balm. A glue stick. And a protractor.

Hang on a minute! A protractor! Now you're talking. In fact, this is exactly what you need to be a top goalkeeper. A protractor can help you measure angles. And angles are very important when it comes to goalkeeping.

I'm not being **obtuse!**

In fact, I'm going to teach you an **acute** way for a goalkeeper to save shots.

Think of it like this. Imagine you're trying to throw a scrunched-up piece of paper into the rubbish bin.

Do you think it would be easier to throw it into a very small bin, with a tiny opening that is barely wider than the scrunched-up paper itself? Or into a massive skip where there's lots of space to aim for? The massive skip would be easier, of course!

Let's say the goal is the bin and the scrunched-up paper is the ball. As a goalkeeper, you want to make life as hard as you can for your opponent, and give them as small a space as possible to get the ball into.

When this goalkeeper stays on the goal line, look at how much of the goal the striker has to aim at. The goalkeeper is allowing space on either side for the striker to shoot at, and this increases the chances of a shot on target beyond the goalkeeper's reach – and therefore a goal.

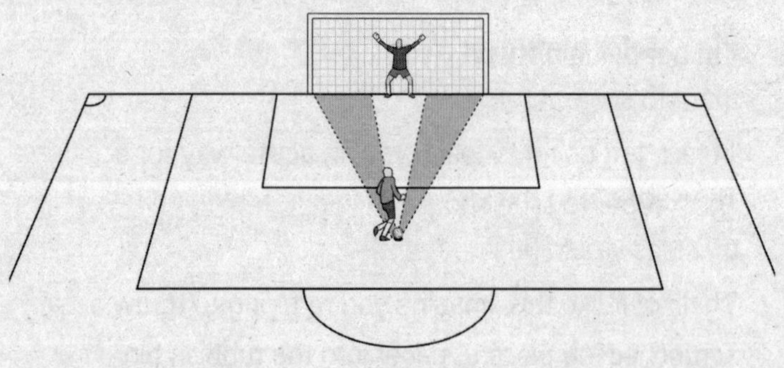

Now look at this goalkeeper, who has come off the goal line to narrow the angles available to the striker to get the ball past the keeper and inside the goalposts. There is now far less room on either side of the goalkeeper for the striker to find the back of the net.

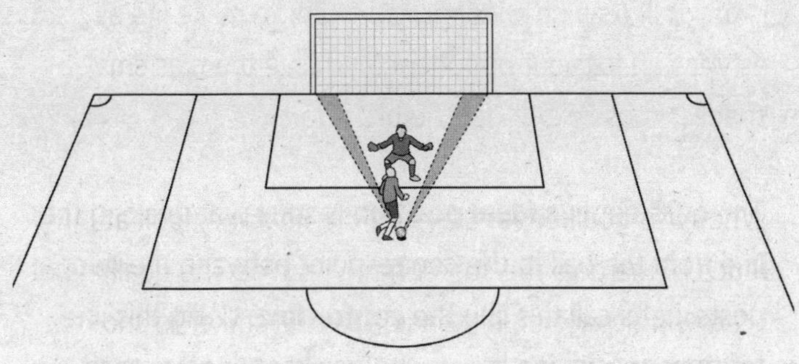

It's usually true that the closer the goalkeeper is to the striker at the time of the shot, the less space there is in the goal for the striker to aim at. This makes it harder for them to score.

The secret is to think about triangles. I told you that triangles would be important!

Imagine a triangle where two corners are the posts, and the third corner is where the ball is.

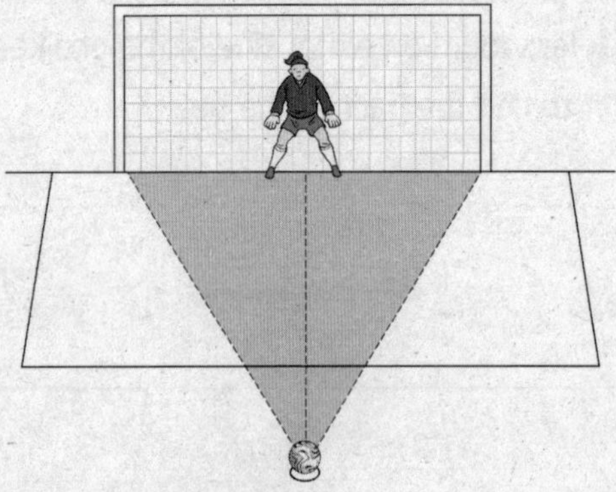

The goalkeeper's **ideal position** is somewhere along the line from the ball to the centre-point between the two posts. Let's call this line the **centre-line**. Using this line for their positioning is how the goalkeeper gives their opponent as little of the goal as possible to aim at – and it means they can cover each corner of the goal equally well. If the ball is on the penalty spot, the centre-line for the goalkeeper will be the centre of the goal.

But when the ball is towards one side of the pitch, the centre-line changes. A new triangle needs to be created, where the goalkeeper can cover the areas inside each post equally well.

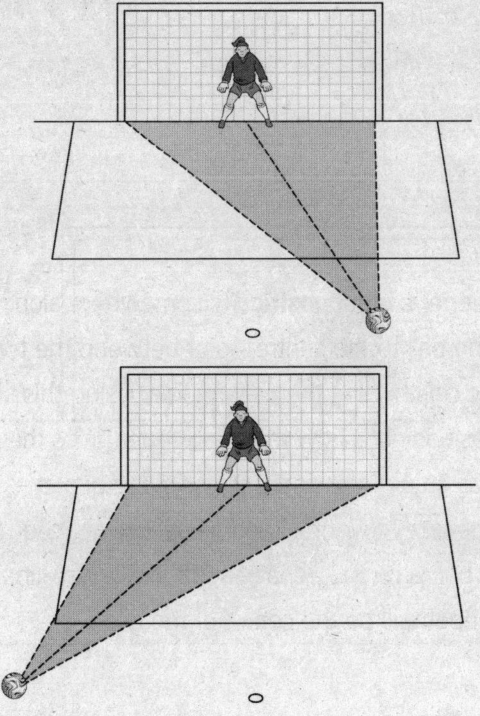

We call these posts the 'near' post and 'far' post, with the near post being the one closest to the ball when a player is shooting or crossing.

For example:

Hi! I'm the post nearest the ball, so I'm the near post!
Hi! I'm the post farthest away from the ball, so I'm the far post!
Near post
Far post
Thanks for always being by my side!
You're far and away my favourite post!

Let's look at these examples together. To help, I have marked the centre of the goal with an X and shown a dotted line to the ball. Can you work out if the goalkeeper is in the right or wrong position?

ONE

TWO

RIGHT or WRONG ?

THREE

RIGHT or WRONG ?

Answer: the goalkeeper is in the right position in image one and image two, but not in image three. Can you see why?

In images one and two, the goalkeeper is standing somewhere along the centre-line.

In image three, the goalkeeper is a long way off the centre line and is giving the opponent a large and unprotected area of the goal to aim for.

The challenge for goalkeepers is that there is no way to mark the centre-line of the goal from any position other than the penalty spot. Unfortunately, protractors are not allowed on the pitch!

Germany goalkeeper Manuel Neuer helped Germany win the 2014 World Cup partly thanks to his expert knowledge of angles.

'If you are very good at maths and trigonometry you can be a good goalkeeper,' says Neuer.

Neuer only conceded five goals in the seven games that Germany played to win the tournament. He was named

Player of the Match in a 2–1 victory over Algeria after a superb display of zonal defence in which he cleared the ball five times and made twenty touches of the ball outside his penalty area. In the quarter-final win over France, Neuer kept out a rising shot from Karim Benzema with his wrist; the ball bounced back with such ferocity that fans thought it had hit the crossbar. And in the final against Argentina, Neuer's speed off his line distracted striker Rodrigo Palacio, who lifted his shot over the top of the goal. 

'The most important basic for the goalkeeper is to have the right position,' Neuer said. '[. . .] You have some marks on the field: the penalty spot, the six-yard box and the corners of the box. You always have to know where your goal is, and the penalty spot is always in the middle; that helps a lot. Pythagoras would have been a good goalkeeper!'

All goalkeepers can do is be aware of where they are in relation to the goalposts, at all times, and to try their best to stay along the centre-line. They should always have that triangle in mind and think about how to make as little space available as possible for the striker to aim towards.

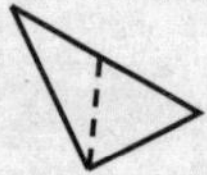

If the ball moves across the pitch to another area, then the goalkeeper must adjust their position accordingly to stay on that centre-line. If the ball is bouncing around in the goal area, and moving from one side to the other, this can be quite tricky. You just need to be ready to leap from side to side to follow the direction of the ball!

SIDEWAYS LEAP DRILL

1. Stand in the set position: knees bent, hands out and feet shoulder-width apart.
2. Have a friend throw the ball to one side of you. Sidestep to the ball and catch it.
3. Quickly come back to the middle and return the ball to the thrower.
4. Repeat on the other side, then go again.
5. Ask the thrower to speed up their throws to get you moving faster.
6. Stay balanced, keep your body low and move quickly.

Now you know where to stand in relation to your goalposts, the next thing you need to think about is where to stand in relation to your goal line – that is, the line of the goal that you are protecting.

If your team has the ball and is in the opposition half, there is no need for you to be standing on your goal line. You can move forward and stand somewhere between the penalty spot and the edge of the goal area. Remember David Raya? He likes to stand on the edge of his area and sometimes even outside it! This can also be helpful if your teammates want to pass the ball back to you.

Again, where you stand will depend on where the ball is – and where it's going.

If the opposition has the ball in their own half and kicks it in your direction, you have a decision to make. Are you going to be able to intercept it before it reaches another opponent? If you can get there, go for it! If not, stay on your centre-line, move into the set position and get ready to make a save. (We'll be covering how to do that in the next chapter.)

Being a master of zonal defence and stopping potential chances before they become actual chances means you have to step away from your goal line sometimes. But it does run one risk: that a player will take a long-distance shot that flies over your head and into the goal because you're not there to defend it. This type of shot is known as a lob. Scoring from a lob requires a lot of skill and is extremely rare.

That's why most goalkeepers believe that stepping away from their goal line is usually worth the risk.

POSITIONING TIPS

- *Always know the location of the goalposts in relation to where you're standing.*
- *Try to stay in the centre-line between the two goalposts and the ball.*
- *Be ready to rush out of the area if needed to stop a potential chance from becoming an actual chance.*
- *Look out for a lob if you are off your goal line.*
- *Remember that triangles are your friend!*

DAYLIGHT LOBBERY

Wimbledon goalkeeper Neil Sullivan was on the receiving end of one of the Premier League's most famous goals: a lob from the half-way line that launched the career of David Beckham back in 1996.

Sullivan was standing near the penalty spot when Beckham, then only twenty-one years old, fired in his super-accurate goal for Manchester United. Sullivan was too far out of his goal to save the brilliant strike, which changed the lives of both players.

Beckham went on to become an England captain and a global icon. Sullivan gave an interview about the goal, which revealed he had a Scottish grandfather. That attracted the attention of the Scotland coach, who called him up to play for Scotland at the 1998 World Cup. Sullivan conceded Beckham's goal, but he ended up achieving his dream too!

Push! Pull! Push! Pull!

What's going on here? Is someone vacuuming in the hallway? No.

Opening lots of drawers to look for something? No.

Trying to defend their goal from a corner kick while surrounded by opposition players? Yes!

A set piece is when the ball is not in play and then the game restarts – like from a corner, a free kick, a penalty or a throw-in.

During a set piece, goalkeepers need to be on their toes and ready for anything. Most of all, they need space. Space to see the ball as it comes closer to the goal. And space to move towards the ball.

The attacking team will do all they can to try to prevent keepers from getting that space, such as:

- Crowding around the goalkeeper during a corner (that's allowed)
- Blocking their view during a free kick (that's allowed)
- Pushing or pulling the goalkeeper so they can't reach the ball (not allowed, but sometimes done anyway)

All these tricks are designed to make it harder for the goalkeeper to make a save.

This is why it's not just about making sure you, as the goalkeeper, are in the right position during a set piece. You also need to make sure your teammates are in the right position to help you manage the situation and get the space you need.

And I'm going to show you how to do this for two different set pieces.

CORNER POSITION

If your opponent has been given a corner, place yourself on the centre of the goal line and take one small step towards the far post. This is because, when you need to react quickly, it's easier to move forwards than backwards. As soon as you see where the corner is heading, you can step forwards if it's going to the near post, and stay back if it's aimed at the far post.

You should also take two small steps away from the goal line and towards the penalty spot. Your job is to dominate as much of the area as you can. Being on your goal line is too far back, as you will be crowded by other players and may not be able to reach the ball with so many people in the way. Stepping off the line gives you a better view of the ball and a better chance of intercepting and catching the cross when it comes in.

Finally, place a teammate right next to the near post, inside the area of the goal. They can help by guarding that part of the goal, and block shots or clear the ball if it comes their way.

FREE-KICK POSITION

If the opponent has a free kick within shooting range of the goal, the goalkeeper could set up a wall.

I don't mean getting some bricks and mortar and quickly building an actual wall! A wall in football refers to a group of defenders who stand next to each other to stop a free kick. They are placed strategically to block part of the goal from the shooter and make it harder for them to score. That way, the goalkeeper only needs to worry about guarding a smaller portion of the goal. This works well if the wall is set up correctly. If not, it can lead to a lot more problems!

The goalkeeper chooses how many players go in the wall. The straighter the angle your opponent is shooting from, the more players you might need in the wall. The exact number could be between two and five, and will also depend on how confident the goalkeeper is feeling.

The players in the wall need to stand close to each other so the ball cannot slip between them. The player on the outside of the wall, closest to the near post, is called the anchor. Once the wall is in position, the goalkeeper or another teammate should quickly stand at the near post to make sure the anchor is blocking a direct shot to that area.

Good wall

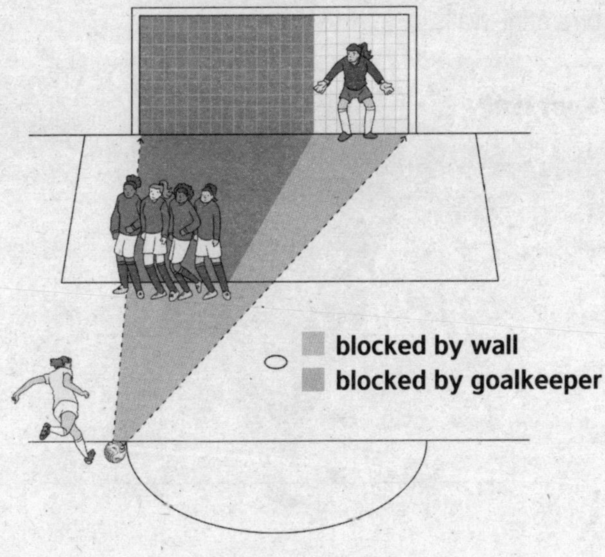

There is another wall option if you want the goal to be extra protected. This will only work if a free kick is in a central area. It's called a split wall, but in fact it's really two mini-walls.

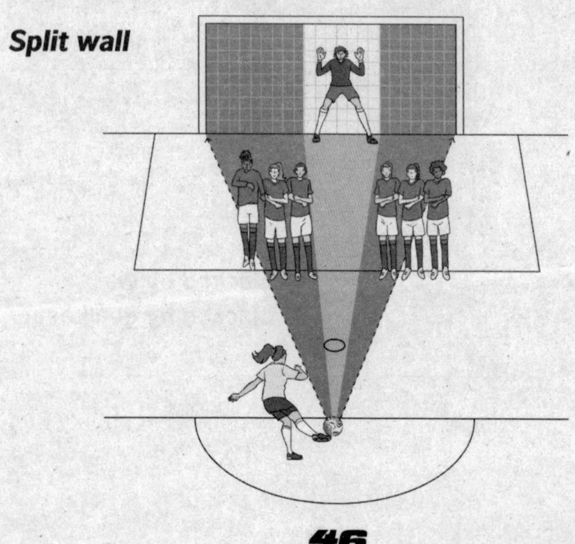

Esteban Andrada, Mexican club Monterrey's Argentinian goalkeeper, used a split wall during the 2025 Club World Cup – and it worked very well! Having two walls made up of four players on each side made it hard for the free-kick taker to place the ball in either corner of the goal. He ended up trying to blast the ball through the centre between the walls, which was exactly where the goalkeeper was standing. It was an easy save! A split wall might be hard to organize, but it can work.

When it comes to a wall, it's always the goalkeeper's choice. And in some cases, it might be easier not to have a wall. For example, if the free kick is being taken a long way from goal and the goalkeeper wants to have a clear view of it. Or if the free kick is out wide and there is no chance of it leading to a direct shot on goal.

A LOW BLOW

Wait a minute, is that a squirrel in the garden . . . doing back-flips? Made you look!

No, let's be serious now.

Hang on! There's a spider on your arm! . . . Made you look again!

It's the oldest trick in the book. Deflecting attention in one direction so we can try to get away with doing something somewhere else. And cheeky strikers try it all the time.

Some of the best free-kick takers in the world use their eyes and body language to make it look like they are aiming for the top corner, and then they aim low instead. They know that players in the wall usually jump up in unison to stop the ball being curled over their heads and into the net. Which leaves a gap below them!

Brazilian Ronaldinho, Portuguese legend Cristiano Ronaldo and Belgium's Kevin De Bruyne have all scored from free kicks by pretending to aim high and then kicking the ball under the wall. What an underhand tactic!

To prevent this, some goalkeepers add an extra player to the wall. That player lies down on their side, facing the goal, behind the wall. They are there to protect the low, under-the-wall shot.

The position is called the 'draught excluder' in England, because those players are like the long object you put on the floor by a door to stop cold air (known as a draught) getting in In Germany, it is called the railway barrier. In Italy, the crocodile. You certainly don't want this under-the-wall tactic to bite you!

HUNGARY FOR SUCCESS

We're going to end this chapter by going back in time.
A long way back! To 1953, when England played a
historic match against Hungary that changed the future of
football.

At the time, England had never lost a match to a non-
British side at their home ground, Wembley Stadium.
Hungary were the 1952 Olympic champions and one of
the best teams in the world. However, no matter how
good they were, no one believed they could beat England
– England! – at Wembley. It turned out they could!

FINAL SCORE:

ENGLAND 3 HUNGARY 6

Not only did Hungary beat England, they thrashed them.
And six months later, Hungary smashed them again,
winning 7–1 in Budapest. It remains England's biggest

ever defeat. The two games forced England to change
their tactics and, for the first time, learn from a foreign
team how to do things differently – a change that helped
them go on to win the 1966 World Cup.

In both matches, it was clear that Hungary's players
were fitter than England's. Their forward players also
used clever movements to find space away from
the English defenders, which created lots of scoring
opportunities. (In that first match, Hungary had thirty-
five shots in total, while England only had five.) And their
goalkeeper did something that was extremely unusual at
the time . . .

In the first match, with Hungary leading 4–2, England
played a long ball – a pass that sends the ball a long
distance, usually from one end of the pitch to the other
– aimed at striker Stan Mortensen. But before he could
reach the ball, Hungary goalkeeper Gyula Grosics was
out of his area and volleying the ball clear. No other
team had a goalkeeper who did this at the time! Most
goalkeepers, including England's Gil Merrick, would stay
close to their goal line and wait for a shot on goal before
getting involved in the game.

Grosics, however, was a goalkeeper whose starting
position was on the edge of the penalty area – and this
was one of the reasons why Hungary were so successful.
When he passed the ball out to his teammates from
there, they were already near the half-way line or even
in the opposition half. He could start attacks before the
opposition was ready.

He was also happy to run out of his area to become
an extra defender. Hungary usually lined up with only
three defenders, and Grosics explained that his precise
role was to act as a fourth defender in the team. Today,
players like Brazilian goalkeeper Ederson and Spanish
goalkeeper Cata Coll use similar tactics – but Grosics was
playing more than seventy years ago!

He felt it was extremely important that the goalkeeper
was integrated with the rest of the team – including
training with them as an outfield player. 'Harmony
between the defenders and the goalkeeper is of the
greatest importance,' he said.

Grosics would have made history had it not been for a
huge rainstorm that happened one July day in 1954.
He played in goal for Hungary in the 1954 World Cup

final against West Germany. Hungary were unbeaten in the previous four years and had already beaten West Germany 8–3 in the group stage of the tournament. They were expected to win again and to be crowned world champions. It did not quite work out like that.

As the rain poured down during the match, the pitch became muddy and slowed down the ball, and the Hungary players kept slipping on the wet turf. West Germany did not have the same problem, as they were wearing boots with built-in studs – the first time a team had done so – to help them keep a grip on the wet pitch. West Germany ended up winning 3–2.

After the tournament, Grosics got into trouble. Hungary's government at the time was very strict. They knew that Grosics was smart and that, before and after matches, he spoke to lots of people from other countries. The government accused him of sharing their secrets and being a spy – even though he wasn't!

Grosics was arrested and banned from playing football for a year. When the ban was up, the government made him play for the army team, Honvéd, and not the team that he wanted to join, which was called Ferencváros.

Grosics died in 2014, but before then, he was finally allowed his moment with Ferencváros. The club arranged a friendly match against Sheffield United and selected Grosics in goal. He was eighty-two years old at the time!

Grosics, wearing his trademark all-black goalkeeper kit, played for Ferencváros for the first few minutes and took a few touches of the ball before he was substituted off to leave the football field one last time.

What we learned in this chapter

David Raya – Being in the right position can prevent potential shots from becoming actual shots.

Manuel Neuer – Being good at maths and trigonometry can help you become a pro goalkeeper.

Neil Sullivan – Don't give up if you concede a goal; you never know what might happen next.

Gyula Grosics – Be brave enough to leave the goal area and integrate with your team!

2
SAVES

You're walking in the park and notice your little sister is about to fall off her scooter. You rush forwards to catch her before she scrapes her arm on the ground. Saaaaave!

Your best friend drops his last mouthful of cupcake at his birthday party. You leap towards him and manage to catch it before it hits the floor. Saaaaave!

Your clumsy dad stretches across the dinner table to get some salt and knocks over a glass of water. Somehow, you reach out and keep it up before it soaks your dinner! Saaaaave!

A goalkeeper's main job is to make saves. The skills needed to catch your sister, grab the falling cupcake and keep your dinner dry are all used by goalkeepers in every game in order to save goals. Anticipation. Speed.

Reactions. Handling skills. So, if you've been in any of these situations before, you could have what it takes to be a top goalkeeper.

In this chapter, we will explore the art of handling the ball and saving goals. I will teach you how to catch the ball, how to dive across the goal and how to improve the speed of your reactions. We will also look at when to catch and when to punch; when to spread and when to smother; and reveal every goalkeeper's favourite letter of the alphabet.

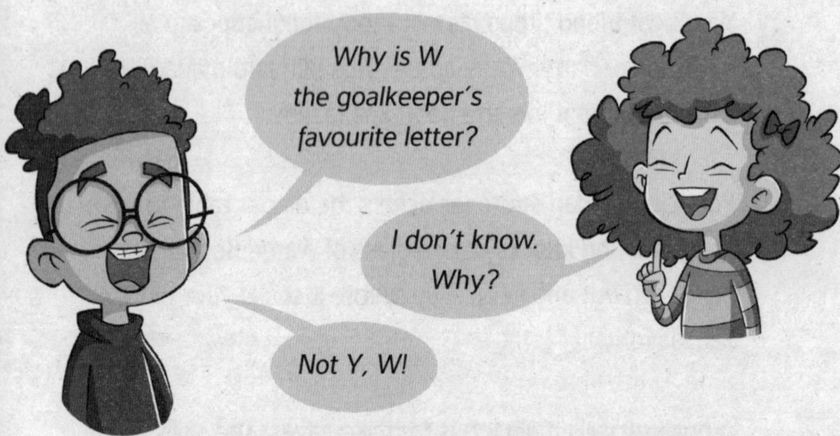

We will also meet the World Cup winner who became a poet. We will get to know the goalkeeper who can dive more than one hundred feet! And discover the goalkeeper who played with one eye.

BACK IN TIME

We know that goalkeepers are special. You wouldn't be reading this book if they weren't, right? Even the Laws of the Game accept this fact. After all, no other player on the pitch is allowed to use their hands on the ball.

But this wasn't always the case! Let's start with a quick history lesson. When football was first played in England in the late 1800s, the rules around goalkeepers were different. To start with, it wasn't even a separate position: any player could catch or knock the ball with their hands. That changed in 1871, when the goalkeeper position was invented.

Here are some of the key dates in goalkeeping history.

1863 – Goalposts are set twenty-four feet apart (the same as they are now) but with no height restriction. There is no designated goalkeeper – any player can catch the ball.

1871 – The goalkeeper position becomes formal: only they can handle the ball to defend the goal, anywhere on the pitch.

1873 – The goalkeeper is not allowed to carry the ball.

1882 – Crossbars are set at eight feet high (the same as they are now), and this is made compulsory on all goals.

1887 – The goalkeeper is only allowed to handle the ball in their own half (as handling the ball in the opposition half is not considered 'defending their goal').

1892 – Goal nets were allowed on all goals.

1909 – The goalkeeper has to wear a different kit to their teammates'.

1912 – The goalkeeper is only allowed to handle the ball in their own penalty area.

1937 – Goal nets become compulsory on all goals.

WHAT'S THE CATCH?

The biggest advantage a goalkeeper has over every other player on the pitch is that they can use their hands. It's called FOOTball, but here we have a player who doesn't have to use just their feet – lucky them! This is only helpful, of course, if you can handle the ball carefully, without any drops or fumbles.

Let me show you how.

Remember the set position? Knees apart, leaning forward, elbows bent and hands out (see page 17).

Now put your fingers up and turn your palms outwards. Make sure your thumbs are close to each other, with the tips pointing diagonally upwards. The position of your thumbs and index fingers (the ones next to your thumbs) should look like the letter W. And what does W stand for?

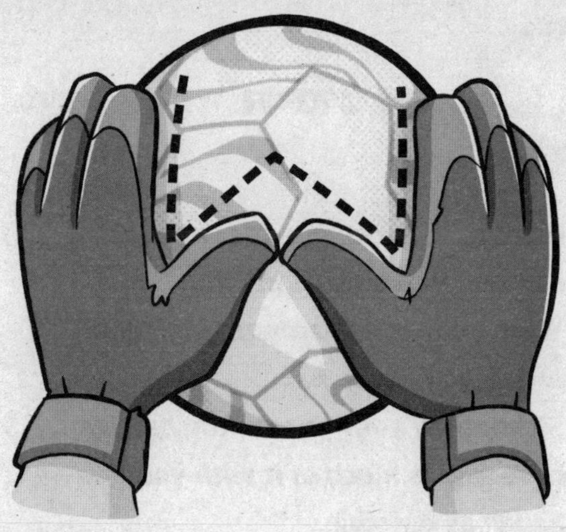

Wally? No!
Wrong? No!
What a save? Yes!

Goalkeepers use the W technique to catch any ball above the waist. Your thumbs add extra support to allow you to catch the ball, while your hands cradle it to absorb a shot or cross's energy. If your wrists are small, bring them closer together and keep the thumbs more upright.

Once the ball is in your hands, gently bring it to your chest for a secure grip. Got it? Thumbs up!

W TIPS

- *Use the W technique for any cross or save above waist height.*
- *Wrap your hands around the middle to top half of the ball.*
- *Strengthen your grip on the ball by covering as much of it with your hands as possible.*

JUMPING

Goalkeepers use the W technique to catch high balls. Using this technique while jumping in the air is tricky to start with, but the more you do it, the more you'll get used to it. Particularly if you're a confident jumper! Here are some drills to improve your jumping skills. Try each one at least five times.

JUMPING DRILLS

• **Pogo jumps – Jump up and down on the spot with your hands on your hips.**

• **Squat jumps – With your hands on your hips, squat then jump up.**

• **Skater jumps – Leap to the left and balance on your left foot, then leap to the right and balance on your right foot.**

• **Kneeling hops – Bend on to one knee and then jump forward and land on both feet. Switch knees!**

ONE SCOOP OR TWO?

What about when the ball arrives along the ground or below the waist?

For stopping low shots, you will need to use the Scoop technique. Who doesn't love a scoop or two? Or three (on special occasions)? Goalkeepers also love a scoop.

Let's try this one together!

Bend down with one knee on the ground, and the heel of your other foot touching that knee. Now put your hands together, with your little fingers side by side. Point the fingers downwards, with your palms facing away from you. Form a ramp with your fingers and palms to guide the low ball into your hands, before pulling it up to your chest. Keep the knee of one leg and heel of the other together behind your hands so the ball doesn't accidentally slip through them if it squirms through your grasp.

Once you have mastered the W and the Scoop, you will have the technique to catch any ball, high or low. It takes some practice, but you'll soon catch on!

HANDLING DRILL

1. Have a friend shoot or throw the ball at you from about eight yards away.

2. Ask them to mix up the height of the shots — some chest high, others lower.

3. Make a quick decision about whether to gather the ball using the W or the Scoop technique.

4. Keep practising until you feel comfortable with both techniques.

THE DEEP DIVER

To quickly reach the corners of the goal, goalkeepers need to dive.

Diving can be a goalkeeper's superpower, allowing them to stretch to their fullest to protect their goal. But diving can also be, well, a bit scary.

No one knows this better than USA goalkeeper Phallon Tullis-Joyce. She is the greatest diver in football history! That's because she has combined her two favourite activities – football and marine biology. When she is not saving goals for the USA women's national team, she is deep-sea diving to a depth of 130 feet – that's about the same width as five full-size football goals!

Tullis-Joyce has a collection of shark teeth. She is a researcher specializing in rockfish. She gives talks to children on how they can live more sustainably to help ocean life. She writes educational stories about the marine world. And on matchdays, to keep her mind calm, she draws images of her favourite fish. It's of-fish-al – Phallon is fin-tastic!

So, how do you start diving like a pro like Tullis-Joyce? Well, whether it's in the water or on the pitch, you need to start slow and steady to get used to the feeling of diving. Then, bit by bit, you can increase the difficulty and try harder dives. When you're a true expert, you can dive really deep . . . or to the far corners!

Here are some drills to help you learn how to dive. We'll start with a warm-up drill to help get your muscles ready to go. Then, once you can manage the kneeling dive, you're ready to try the standing dive.

WARM-UP DRILL

1. Place four different-coloured cones about six metres apart in a square.

2. Create a starting point mark in the centre of one side of the square.

3. Have a friend shout out the colour of one of the cones.

4. Sidestep or sprint diagonally to that colour cone and then back to your mark.

5. Continue for one minute.

KNEELING DIVE DRILL

1. Kneel on the ground.

2. Hold your hands out in front of your body with your palms facing inwards.

3. Have a friend kick the ball low to one side of you.

4. While still in the kneeling position, lean and then dive towards the ball, keeping your lower hand close to the ground.

5. When the lower hand is behind the ball, put your upper hand on top to control it.

6. Repeat until you save three in a row.

STANDING DIVE DRILL

1. Stand in the set position.

2. Have a friend kick the ball low to one side of you.

3. Take one diagonal step in the direction of the ball, pushing off with your standing leg.

4. As you leap to leave the ground, extend your arms towards the ball to maximize your reach and add momentum to the dive.

5. Keep your body low and horizontal to the ground.

6. Use your lower hand to stop the ball and your upper hand to press it down against the ground to control it.

7. Repeat until you save three in a row.

Gordon Banks is considered to be one of the best, if not the best, English goalkeeper of all time.

- He was in goal when England won the 1966 World Cup.
- He was named FIFA Goalkeeper of the Year six years running.
- He was in goal when Stoke won the 1972 League Cup, the only trophy in their history.
- He was named Goalkeeper of the Year after playing a full season with only one eye.

But Banks is most famous for one save he made during the 1970 World Cup. A save so brilliant, so unexpected, so gravity-defying, that it showed the world just how extraordinary goalkeeping could be.

It also showed that to make an amazing save, you don't necessarily need to catch the ball. Because Banks did not catch the ball. He didn't even hold on to the ball. He tipped the ball over the crossbar!

The save that Banks made is still known today as the Save of the Century.

Going into the 1970 World Cup, England were reigning world champions and were facing tournament favourites Brazil in the group stage. The game was played in boiling-hot conditions on a dry, hard pitch in Mexico.

After ten minutes, winger Jairzinho dribbled the ball into the area. Banks spotted a forward player making a run towards the near post, so he sidestepped in that direction. But Jairzinho crossed the ball deeper, past the penalty spot and there, eight yards out, was Brazil striker Pelé. The best player in the world. Pelé headed the ball down into the ground and towards the bottom corner of the goal. He was so confident he would score that he even shouted, 'Gol!' after he made contact with the ball.

Banks, though, was alert. Despite his movements towards the near post, he tracked the ball and was able to dive at full length in the other direction, twisting his body backwards and flicking the ball up and over the crossbar with his outstretched fingers.

Pelé was all set to celebrate. He could not believe what he had seen.

'Banks came from nowhere, and he did something I didn't feel was possible,' Pelé said. 'He appeared in my sight, like a kind of blue phantom. I can't believe how he moved so far, so fast.'

As we know from the previous chapter, you can only make great saves if you're in the correct position. Banks was tracking the ball and knew exactly where he was at all times in relation to the goal.

England lost the game 1–0, but Pelé never forgot that save. He told Banks it was the best save he'd ever seen, and this began a friendship between the two players that lasted for decades.

When he was thirty-two, Banks was in an accident that left him blinded in his right eye. But he did not give up goalkeeping.

'Goalkeeping is about geometry [we learned that in chapter one, Gordon!] and with one eye, I set out to re-educate myself about angles and positioning,' he said.

Because he found it harder to track the speed of the ball and to spot other players to the side of him as well as in front, he took a break from playing professionally and did some coaching. After a few years, he went back to playing: he moved to the USA and played for a team called Fort Lauderdale Strikers. They won the league in 1977, and he was named Goalkeeper of the Year!

GAMES TIME!

Banks once shared a training tip that helped improve his goalkeeping abilities. He would play games with a ball smaller than a football to test and improve his reflexes (the fast-reaction movements your body makes without you thinking about it). Goalkeepers need good reflexes because they always have to be ready to react in an instant to shots or headers on their goal.

Banks loved table tennis because he had to respond quickly to the movements of the small ball. He also liked throwing a tennis ball against a wall and catching it. First, he'd throw softly, and then he'd start throwing it harder.

Banks said that once he was used to playing with a smaller ball, it became so much easier to play with a bigger one. His practice routines sharpened his reflexes – and helped him keep out Pelé's header! Imagine trying to stop a Pelé effort with a table-tennis ball, though . . . Now that would be really tricky!

GIVE THIBAUT RESPECT!

The 2022 Champions League final pitted Liverpool against Real Madrid. It was an exciting game, and Liverpool attacked extremely well, creating lots of chances to score! In total, they had twenty-three efforts on goal.

But they were up against Thibaut Courtois, a goalkeeper who was at the top of his game. Courtois made nine saves in all, the most ever recorded in a Champions League final. Liverpool never found a way past him, and Real Madrid won the final 1–0.

After the game, Courtois said he was determined to prove himself, because a magazine had recently listed the top ten goalkeepers in the world and had left his name out.

'I needed to win a final for my career, for all the hard work, to put respect on my name. I don't think I get enough respect,' he said.

He certainly got respect after that match! One Spanish goalkeeper said that Courtois was 'without doubt, the best goalkeeper I have ever seen', and called him 'the Messi or Ronaldo of goalkeeping'.

Courtois is a master of handling the ball – not only saving shots, but holding on to the ball too. His catching ability is exceptional. He has perfect technique when it comes to the W and the Scoop. The saves Courtois made in that final also showed off his other main talents, which make for a winning combination:

1. Anticipation: his ability to react before something happens
2. Reflexes: his extremely quick reactions to shots just after they are fired in

Courtois was born with an extra advantage: his genes. These are the characteristics that you get from your parents, like eye colour, the shape and size of your facial features or height. In his case, his parents, who were both semi-professional volleyball players, passed on genes for extremely large hands and a wide arm span. (They also passed this on to Thibaut's sister, who played volleyball for Belgium.) This is incredibly useful for claiming the ball, as it means he can reach to the far corners of the goal, and it helps him catch crosses, whether they are high or low.

Most people have an arm span that's about the same as their height.

MOST PEOPLE:

But Courtois's arm span of 209 centimetres is longer than his height, which is 200 centimetres! Let's hope he thanked his mum and dad for passing on those genes!

THIBAUT COURTOIS:

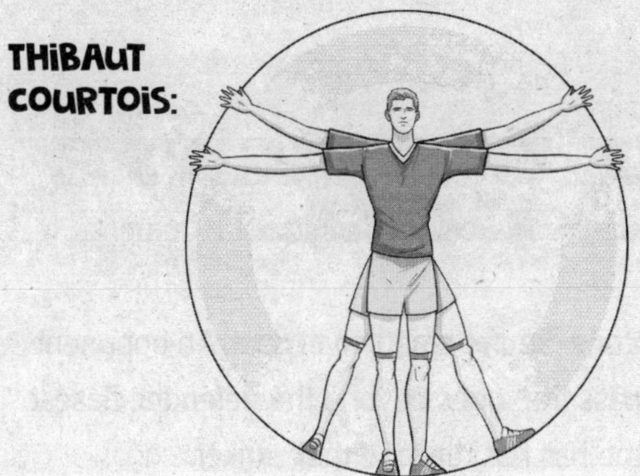

REACTiONS DRiLL

1. Stand on the goal line and face the goal, not the pitch.

2. Have a friend stand eight yards away with a ball at their feet.

3. When the friend says 'Turn', spin to face them.

4. The friend will then shoot quickly for you to try to make a save.

5. Turn around again and repeat.

THE ULTIMATE DUEL

Picture the scene. You're standing in goal. An opponent has made a pass that goes beyond the defender closest to you, and the ball has reached their striker.

You're the only person standing between the striker and the goal. The striker is running towards you. There's you, defending the goal. And the striker, determined to put the ball into the net. This scenario is known as a one-on-one (because there's one striker and one goalkeeper), and it is one of the hardest situations for a goalkeeper. (Obviously, a two-on-one, with two strikers, is even harder!)

The advantage is almost entirely with the striker, who has possession of the ball and, more importantly, knows what their next move will be. The goalkeeper's job is to predict that next move while covering as much of the goal as possible. Or they might decide to try to influence the striker to aim for a certain spot – either by pointing in one direction or leaving a little gap on one side to tempt the striker to aim there.

Do you remember the one-on-one that Argentina goalkeeper Emiliano Martínez saved in the last few seconds of the 2022 World Cup final? (Go back to page 2 if you need a reminder!)

Martínez had spent years preparing for that moment. He knew exactly what to do and when to do it. How to adopt the right body shape. How to move at the right second. How to anticipate where Kolo Muani would shoot. Even how to position himself in a certain way to persuade Kolo Muani to kick the ball where he wanted it to go.

In this case, Martínez left a little bit of space open by the near post – not too much, but just enough to tempt Kolo Muani to aim for that area.

England goalkeeper Hannah Hampton had a similar moment during the Euro 2025 quarter-final against Sweden. With England losing 2–0, Sweden winger Fridolina Rolfö was through on goal. Hampton waited to make her move. At just the right moment, she stepped forward to make the goal smaller for Rolfö, who shot towards her near post. Hampton timed it perfectly and dived to her left to make the important save. (England and Sweden ended up drawing 2–2, before England won the penalty shoot-out with more Hampton heroics!)

Now it's time to explore how these two goalkeepers made their decisions during these tough one-on-one situations, and how you can make the right decisions too!

In a scenario where a goalkeeper is one-on-one with a striker, they have four options: to wait, to spread, to block or to smother.

Making the right pick depends on lots of things, including:

The ball

- Where is the ball in relation to the goal? Is it a long way out? Is it coming at a wide angle?
- How fast is the ball travelling? Can I, or a defender, get to the ball before the striker?
- Is the ball bouncing at an awkward height, or is it on the ground?

The striker

- Where is the striker in relation to the goal? Are they a long way out or close?

- From what direction is the striker running on to the ball? Are they central or coming from a wide position?
- Is the striker right-footed and is the ball on their right foot (or the other way round)? If they want to move the ball on to their stronger foot, will that give me more time to make a decision?
- How skilful is this particular striker?
- Has this striker had a similar one-on-one with me before, and what did they do?

My defenders

- How close are they to the striker?
- Can they catch up to put the striker under pressure and distract them?

DECISION TIME

In a one-on-one, the most important factor in deciding which tactic to use is the ball's distance from the goal. If the ball is closer to the goal, you should use one tactic. If the ball is further away, you should use a different one. Let's see some examples.

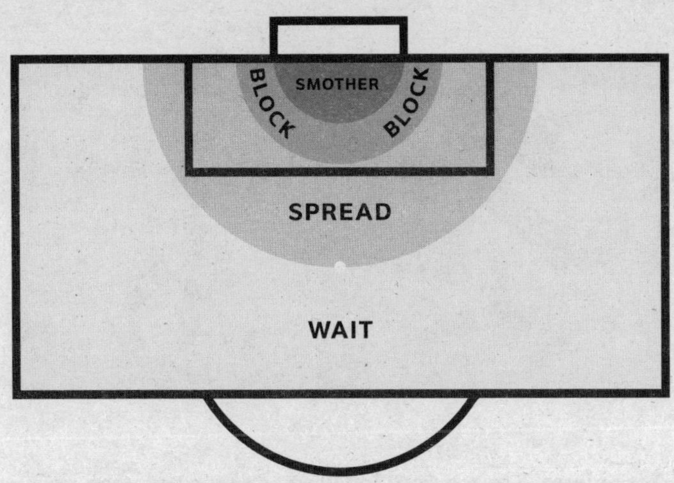

Distance from goal: More than 13 yards

Ball position: Anywhere beyond the penalty spot but still in the penalty area

Tactic: Wait

Technique: Come out a little bit and stand tall, in the set position, but do not dive straight away, because the striker still has a lot to do. Waiting will encourage the striker to make the next move, and means you aren't committing to a challenge too early. The striker might choose to bring the ball closer to goal, which could then change your tactic or allow a defender to make a tackle. Sometimes waiting and not rushing to make a decision is the best choice!

Distance from goal: 7–13 yards

Ball position: Central, between the area of the goalposts

Tactic: Spread

Technique: Stretch your legs out as far as they can go, and do the same with your hands. You are trying to take up as much space as possible to give the striker very little room to get the ball past you.

Distance from goal: Close, up to 6 yards
Ball position: Wide of the goal, outside the area of the goalposts
Tactic: Block
Technique: Drop on to one knee and use the heel of your standing foot to close the gap between your legs so the ball can't get through there. Stretch out your arms and have your body face the ball.

Distance from goal: Very close, within 3 yards

Ball position: Centre, within the area of the goalposts

Tactic: Smother

Technique: Dive to put your hands on the ball, with your legs to the side. Lead with your hands and protect your head by keeping it out of the way of the ball or the striker.

Can you work out which tactic Martínez and Hampton used to make their important one-on-one saves?

As the ball was further away from goal, they both chose to wait before making their stops. But if the ball had been closer to the goal, they might have chosen a different tactic.

THE PUNCH THAT INSPIRED A LEGEND

Italian goalkeeper Gigi Buffon was twelve years old when he decided he wanted to be a goalie. He was at his grandmother's apartment watching Cameroon beat Argentina in a 1990 World Cup match, and he was captivated by the Cameroon goalkeeper Thomas N'Kono. Even though the match was played in searing Italian heat, N'Kono looked cool in a long green jumper with a pink collar. Then Argentina won a corner. And what happened next changed Buffon's life.

As the corner was swung in, N'Kono ran towards the ball and PUNCHED it thirty yards away from the goal. That was it: the moment Buffon knew what he wanted to do with his life. He did not simply want to be a goalkeeper; he wanted to be a goalkeeper like N'Kono – bold and courageous. Buffon said that he was inspired by N'Kono's artistry, style and soul.

Buffon went on to become one of the most successful goalkeepers in football history. He is currently the goalkeeper with the most international appearances of all time, having played 176 times for Italy. He won ten Serie A league titles with Juventus. And he helped guide Italy to success in the 2006 World Cup, as they won a penalty shoot-out in the final.

When Buffon set an Italian league record for going over 970 minutes (ten and a half games) without conceding a goal, he wrote two poems to celebrate. One poem was dedicated to all of his Juventus teammates, in which he thanked them for helping him defend the goal. He named every player and added a short sentence about why he was grateful to each of them. For example, he said he appreciated centre-back Giorgio Chiellini because he never ever gave up.

The other poem was dedicated to the goal itself – an object that he felt truly passionate about. Buffon wrote that the first time he stopped looking the goal in the face (because he was the keeper, and had his back to it) was the day that he started to love the goal. He vowed to always protect it.

Buffon's passion and dedication to his role inspired him throughout his twenty-eight-year career. And it all started back on that hot summer's day, watching N'Kono's punch on TV in his grandmother's apartment!

PUNCHING TIPS

Catching the ball is usually a better option than punching it because that way you get to keep possession. A punch could end up sending the ball to the opposition. The best time to punch the ball is if there are many people around you and you're not confident that you can catch it. So, if you do find yourself in a situation where you need to punch the ball away, here's what you can do:

1. *Make your hand into a fist with your thumb pressed against the sides of your fingers (not tucked under them).*

2. If you want to do a two-handed punch, put both fists close together to create a larger surface area to hit the ball with.

3. Before the punch, place your hands close to your body, elbows to the side, and then push through the ball to direct it as far away as possible.

4. Extend your arm or arms to full length after making contact with the ball.

5. Avoid using an open palm. You want to punch, not slap!

PUNCHING DRILL

1. Kneel down and have a friend stand about six yards away from you.

2. Ask the friend to throw a ball towards you above your head.

3. With two hands, try to punch the ball as far away as possible.

4. Ask the friend to move back a few steps.

5. Stand on your feet and repeat the exercise.

6. Now try it with another friend standing near you, so you can practise punching with other players around.

7. Never punch any players!

What we learned in this chapter

Phallon Tullis-Joyce – Diving is a superpower once you learn how to master it.

Gordon Banks – Playing games with smaller balls will improve your performance on the pitch.

Thibaut Courtois – Long arms are helpful, but good reflexes are more important.

Thomas N'Kono – Punch the ball, not the players!

Gigi Buffon – Remember, your main job is always to protect the goal.

3
PASSING

Even though goalkeepers are allowed to use their hands, more than 80 per cent of their actions during a match involve them kicking and passing the ball. Football today requires goalkeepers to be skilled with the ball at their feet so they can:

- Control passes (which means collect and gain control of the ball) from teammates
- Pass well to start attacks
- Dribble around opponents trying to tackle them

Goalkeepers are now more part of the team than ever before. Their role on the pitch is so important to how teams play overall that one coach, a Dutchman called Frans Hoek, who we will meet later in this chapter, wants their name changed to goalplayers so they are more similar to their teammates.

In this chapter, we will chart the journey of how goalkeepers became goalplayers. And we will learn all about the skill of passing to your teammates, including when to pass long, pass short or throw the ball. You will also discover how passing became the goalkeeper's superpower. What a way to pass the time!

Along the way, we will meet:

- The Swiss coach who worried football was too boring
- The Dutch goalkeeper who wore the number eight shirt
- The Spanish coach who celebrated when his team let in a goal
- The Iranian shepherd who broke a world record

And we will discover why the bottom of a goalkeeper's boot could be the most important part of their kit.

Let's get stuck in!

THE RULE CHANGE

Switzerland's Daniel Jeandupeux was the attack-minded coach of French side Caen when he wrote a letter to a friend in December 1990 that changed the role of the goalkeeper forever.

A few months earlier, Jeandupeux had watched West Germany beat Argentina 1–0 in the 1990 World Cup final. That World Cup was the lowest-scoring in history, and FIFA called the final 'a dreadful advertisement for the game of football'. The games were low on excitement and high on time-wasting. In a word: boooooooring!

In Ireland's 0–0 draw with Egypt, for example, goalkeeper Packie Bonner held the ball in his hands for a total of six minutes throughout the game (not all in one go!). Teams who scored first, or those who were desperate to avoid letting in a goal, would frequently pass the ball back to their goalkeeper, who would then use the following tactic to waste time:

- Pick up the ball
- Bounce the ball a few times
- Roll the ball to a defender
- Receive the ball back from a defender
- Pick it up again
- Repeat

During one match, Jeandupeux calculated how long each player had possession of the ball for. His findings troubled him. Whenever any team, including his, was a goal ahead, one player always had more possession than anyone else: the goalkeeper.

Jeandupeux wrote to his friend Walter Gagg, who was head of FIFA's technical committee, a group that looks at ways to improve the game.

Jeandupeux explained that his goalkeeper at Caen held the ball for nearly seven minutes in total during one match, which accounted for almost half of the time his team had possession. He also calculated that waiting for a ball at throw-ins wasted seventeen minutes in one game!

Jeandupeux came up with three suggestions for how to improve the sport and make it more of an enjoyable experience for fans.

1. *The goalkeeper should only have three seconds to release the ball when he has taken it with his hands.*
2. *The goalkeeper should not be allowed to pick the ball up with his hands if it is kicked to him by a teammate.*
3. *Keeping seven or eight balls around the edge of the pitch could accelerate the restart of the game at throw-ins.*

The technical committee were convinced by
Jeandupeux's letter. And after a successful trial in the
1991 Under-17 World Championship, his second rule
suggestion became official. No goalkeeper was allowed
to pick up a pass from their teammate. This was called
'the backpass rule'.

At the start, the new rule caused chaos for goalkeepers
who were used to picking up the ball. On the first day
of the Premier League season in 1992, three teams let
in goals because of poor backpasses or because the
goalkeepers struggled to respond to the backpasses.

That opening weekend, Wimbledon defender Roger
Joseph under-hit a pass back to his goalkeeper and
Leeds forward Lee Chapman pounced to score. During
another match, Chelsea goalkeeper Dave Beasant
responded to a backpass, but he miskicked it, and the
ball went straight to Ipswich striker Nick Henry to score.
In a third match, Arsenal captain Tony Adams gave
the ball away because his goalkeeper did not want
to receive a pass from him, and that allowed Norwich
striker Mark Robins to nip in and score.

One month later, Sheffield United goalkeeper Simon Tracey was sent off after a disastrous effort at using his feet during a match against Tottenham. He tried to dribble round an opponent inside the six-yard box, but ended up out of position on the side of the pitch, where he lost control of the ball, and it went out of play. A Tottenham player went to throw the ball back in immediately, but Tracey was still on the side of the pitch and nowhere near the goal. Just as the player picked up the ball, Tracey rugby-tackled him to the ground to stop him taking the throw. The referee had no option but to show him a yellow card. As it was his second yellow card of the game, he was sent off.

'I had a lack of technique,' said Tracey. Although he admitted, 'It's probably one of the best rules that has come in.'

Why? The rule change was good for many reasons:

- It cut down on time-wasting.
- It sped up the game, because there were fewer breaks in play.
- It stopped goalkeepers from just kicking the ball from their hands as far as they could, from one end of the pitch to the other, and meant more dribbling and passing could happen in midfield.

And it turned goalkeepers from outsiders who were often seen as separate from the team into important players! They are now judged almost as much on their ability to pass as they are on their ability to save goals.

Jeandupeux's other two suggestions were also partly adopted, although not until much later. In 1998, a rule was passed that goalkeepers could only hold on to the ball for six seconds. In 2025, the time limit was extended to eight seconds, and if the goalkeeper went over that time, a corner would be awarded to the opposition.

His idea to place balls around the edge of the pitch to speed up throw-ins was also adopted. It's called the multi-ball system. It was first used in the World Cup in 2006 and in the Premier League in 2022.

GAME ON!

With the new backpass rule, goalkeepers quickly needed to learn how to play with the ball at their feet. The best way to do this was to train with the outfield players in their team so they could start playing like them. They needed to practise controlling the ball, passing at different angles and distances, and learning where teammates would be at certain moments.

The best way for goalkeepers to deal with backpasses is to pass the ball straight to another teammate. When that's not possible, the next best thing to do is to kick the ball away from the goal and away from the opposition. Here's a drill you can practise to get comfortable with this.

BACKPASS DRILL

1. Have a friend pass the ball to you at speed from about 8 metres away.

2. Take one touch to control the ball, and the next touch to pass it diagonally away from your position.

3. Repeat until you are comfortable passing diagonally to both sides.

4. Now repeat the drill, but this time you only have one touch.

5. Pass diagonally to either side, or kick it long and with height.

6. Avoid kicking the ball back to where it originally came from.

AHEAD OF THE CURVE

If you look at the squad list for the Netherlands for the 1974 World Cup, it's clear that the Dutch had a different view when it came to goalkeepers.

Number 1 was Ruud Geels, a striker
Number 2 was Arie Haan, a midfielder
Number 3 was Wim van Hanegem, a midfielder
Number 4 was Kees van Ierssel, a defender

Can you work out how the Dutch were numbering their players? It was in alphabetical order! (With the exception of their best player, Johan Cruyff, who always wore his favourite number fourteen jersey.)

Because of this numbering system, the goalkeeper, Jan Jongbloed, ended up wearing the number eight shirt. All the other goalkeepers in the competition wore the number one shirt! This was proof that the Netherlands saw the role of the goalkeeper as being like any other player.

And this was a belief that Cruyff continued to hold when he became a coach at Ajax in the 1980s and Barcelona in the late 1980s and 1990s. He insisted that the goalkeepers needed to be as good at passing as their teammates. He had read one of the first books written about goalkeeping, called *So Now You Are a Goalkeeper*, and liked it so much that he hired one of its authors, Frans Hoek, to coach the goalies in his team. Hoek was one of the first specialist goalkeeping coaches ever hired, and both Cruyff's and Hoek's ideas continue to be huge influences in football and goalkeeping today.

The most important idea for Hoek was that goalkeepers were part of the team and therefore needed to train alongside their teammates. After one month of training alone with the goalkeepers at Ajax, he asked Cruyff to bring the outfield players to join the sessions too. He had noticed that the goalkeeper, Stanley Menzo, didn't know when to come out of the area to claim the ball and when to stay in his area. The goalkeepers were training separately from everyone else, so there was no opportunity to practise this.

'How can he improve when it only happens in the game?' Hoek asked.

Cruyff understood and agreed. So Hoek developed a training session that was similar to what would happen in a real match. He had the players line up as they would in a real game, having to defend through-balls played to the strikers. This helped Menzo learn when he should rush from his area to intercept the ball and when he should stay, based on what the rest of his team were doing and where they were standing. It helped improve everyone's game.

By training more as a team, they became more of a team.

So when the backpass rule came into effect in 1992, Ajax were perfectly placed to take advantage. Their goalkeepers knew what to do with the ball, while opposition goalkeepers did not.

Thanks to Hoek's creative methods, it was no surprise that, in 1995, Ajax won the Champions League. Their goalkeeper was a young Dutchman called Edwin van der Sar, who was brilliant at playing with the ball at his feet. He would go on to join Manchester United and win four Premier League titles and another Champions League.

Hoek thinks it's time to change the name of the goalkeeper position. 'Goalkeeper does not cover it anymore. It is about more than keeping it out of the net . . . The goalplayer needs to defend by keeping the ball out of the net and attack with the build-up. They are almost the same as the other players – the only difference is that they are wearing gloves and a different-coloured shirt.'

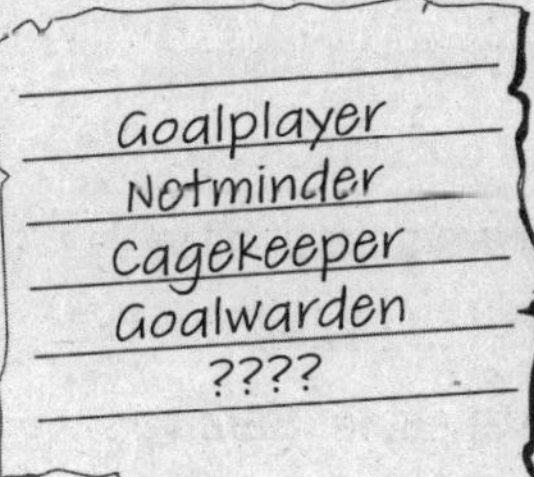

Do you like the term goalkeeper? Do you prefer goalplayer? Or is there another word that would be even better?

Did you know? Argentina adopted the same numbering system as the Dutch in 1978 and, coincidentally, beat the Netherlands in the World Cup final that year. In the final, neither goalkeeper wore the number one. In goal for the Netherlands was Jongbloed, wearing number eight, and for Argentina it was Ubaldo Fillol, wearing number five.

PEP TALK

In 2011, Spanish football's greatest rivals, Real Madrid and Barcelona, played each other in a league match. And people could not believe what they were seeing. After just twenty seconds, Barcelona's Spanish goalkeeper Victor Valdés passed the ball to the left side of his goal area, where his teammate, Frenchman Éric Abidal, was waiting. The pass was mishit and went straight to Real Madrid's Argentinian winger Ángel Di María. The ball eventually fell to Madrid and France striker Karim Benzema, who scored to put his team ahead within the first minute.

As the Real Madrid fans erupted with joy, eyes were drawn to the Barcelona coach Pep Guardiola on the touchline. He was cheering too! He was clapping Valdés for trying to pass the ball out, and for not just smashing the ball down the pitch as far as he could. This isn't easy when the opposition are putting a keeper under lots of pressure – known as pressing.

Guardiola had previously played under Cruyff at Barcelona, and he adopted the same approach to goalkeeping: he wanted keepers to be an extra outfield player, always looking to be involved in the game and to start attacks. He was not at all cross with Valdés when Barcelona conceded that goal. He wanted him to continue playing like that! He believed that this method would lead to winning more matches – and he was right.

Barcelona went on to win the match 3–1, and they won many more trophies under Guardiola (fourteen in just three years).

Guardiola then moved to Manchester City in 2016 and helped them win numerous Premier League titles, as well as the 2023 Champions League. His influence has been felt throughout English football, where almost every team now asks their goalkeepers to pass like an outfield player.

Guardiola's preferred goalkeeper at Manchester City was a Brazilian called Ederson, who was just as skilled as his teammates at passing the ball.

'Sometimes I am able to step up and play almost as a third centre-back, to help the ball come out from the back,' said Ederson. 'It's a big responsibility because one mistake can cost us a goal. But I'm ready.'

Ederson was a brilliant passer. He still holds the record for the most assists by a goalkeeper in the Premier League. That's another opportunity for Pep to celebrate – and this time, for the right reason!

THE FOUR TECHNIQUES

Now we know how valuable goalkeepers who can pass the ball and play like an outfield player are, the next question is how should goalkeepers pass and who should they pass to?

There are four main passing techniques for a goalkeeper to master. Let's break them down and understand how you can improve each one.

1. RECEIVING BACKPASSES

Remember: Don't pick up the ball!

Decision to make: Should you pass with the first touch (if you are being pressed) or control the ball (if you have time)?

Things to practise:

- Body shape – you need to be side-on when the ball arrives to allow you space to control the ball and then pass it
- Looking around – you should always know where your teammates are so you can find them with your pass
- Passing with your weaker foot – you might need to use it, depending on where the ball ends up!

2. KICKS FROM THE HAND

Remember: You can kick long and quickly when the ball is in your hands.

Decision to make: Should you volley, drop-kick or side-volley the ball? (This depends on which technique you prefer and are most accurate with.)

Things to practise:

- Spotting your target – you must always make sure your teammate is expecting the ball so they can run on to it
- Technique – once you get the technique right, the power and distance will follow
- Timing – you need to hit the ball at the right moment – not too late or early – for maximum impact

Did you know? Netherlands goalkeeper Eddy Treijtel was playing for Feyenoord against Sparta Rotterdam in 1970 when his goal kick accidentally hit and killed a seagull flying above the stadium. Sparta fans claimed the seagull supported their team and was trying to block the kick on purpose. The seagull is now stuffed and kept in the Feyenoord club museum as a memento.

3. THROWS

Remember: Don't release or drop the ball before you are ready!

Decision to make: Should you do an under-arm roll (if your teammates are close by) or an overarm throw (if they are further away, usually near the touchline)?

Things to practise:

- Speed – if a nearby teammate is alert and ready, a quick under-arm roll towards them can start an attack before the opposition is ready

- Distance – you need to know how far you can throw the ball to work out if you will be able to reach your teammates across the pitch

- Positioning – you might need to run to the edge of your area before throwing the ball to make some extra distance

THROWING STONES

Dal Paran is a game that children play in Iran. It involves throwing stones as far as you can, and the winner is the person who can hurl a stone the longest distance. An Iranian kid called Alireza Beiranvand was really good at Dal Paran. So good, in fact, that he ended up as a world-record holder!

Beiranvand was the son of sheep farmers, and he and his family were constantly having to move around to places where there was enough grass to feed their sheep. Because drought and dust storms were a regular part of life, they moved home a lot. Beiranvand made friends with other children wherever he went by playing Dal Paran with them.

He dreamed of becoming a goalkeeper one day and, as a teenager, defied his parents' wishes and moved to the capital city, Tehran, to find a football club. After working in a pizzeria and a car wash, he finally found a job as goalkeeper for a team called Naft.

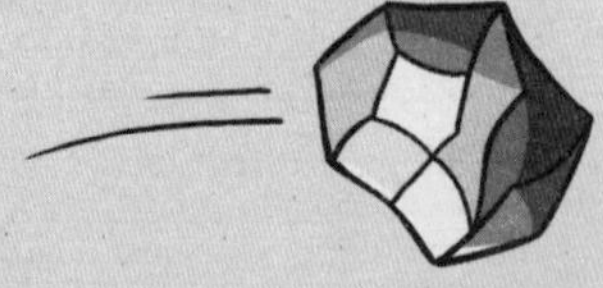

Here, the skills he had developed over the years by playing Dal Paran made him famous. In one game, he caught a cross, ran to the edge of the area and threw the ball nearly seventy metres, almost to the edge of the opposition area. With his first touch, the Naft striker scored a goal, and Beiranvand had the assist – from a throw!

Beiranvand's talent for throwing became legendary and before long, he was called up to play for the Iran national team. He then broke the world record for the longest throw in a competitive match when he hurled the ball over sixty metres in an international game against South Korea in 2016. The shepherd became even more famous when, at the 2018 World Cup, he saved a penalty taken by . . . Cristiano Ronaldo!

Beiranvand's long throws were always a dangerous attacking weapon. Even when his team were defending a corner, the opposition were nervous he would catch the ball and create an attacking opportunity within seconds. That's the power of a long throw – and the beauty of Dal Paran!

4. GOAL KICKS

Remember: This is a good opportunity to keep possession for your team!

Decision to make: Should you kick short (if nearby teammates are unmarked) or long (if no one nearby is free)?

Things to practise:

- Talking – you need to be able to communicate with your teammates to know where they want the ball and if they're ready

- Complete the motion – keep moving your leg in the direction of the ball after you have kicked it, rather than abruptly stopping on impact. This is known as the follow-through.
- Scanning the pitch – it's important to spot your opponents so you know where to avoid sending the ball

GOAL KICK TIPS

1. **Make sure the ball is on the ground and stationary.**
2. **Approach the ball at a slight angle.**
3. **Choose a target to aim for.**
4. **Place your non-kicking foot alongside but slightly behind the ball, pointing at your target.**
5. **Keep your body slightly leaned back to help give the ball some height.**
6. **Hit the lower half of the ball with your laces. (The ball will stay low if you hit the middle of the ball and go high if you hit the bottom of or underneath the ball.)**

7. **Follow through with the kicking foot, continuing in the kick direction.**
8. **Look at the target after contact to make sure your aim is accurate.**
9. **Practise with different heights – sometimes high, sometimes low.**

GOAL-KICK DRILL

1. Place some cones at different distances away from the goal.

2. Stand in goal.

3. Kick the ball and aim to land it as close to the targets as possible.

4. Repeat, aiming to land the ball closer to the targets every time.

THE LONG AND SHORT OF IT

Another important law change was introduced for goalkeepers in 2019. Before then, all their goal kicks had to leave the goal area. The new rule stated that goalkeepers can pass to a teammate inside the area from a goal kick (and all opponents must be outside the area).

This means goalkeepers now have another decision to make when taking a goal kick. Do they pass the ball:

Inside the area, which guarantees their team keeps possession, but leaves the ball near their goal?
OR
Outside the area, which lowers the chances that their team keeps possession, but gets the ball nearer the opposition goal?

What would you pick?

Your choice might depend on a few things, including which teammate you are passing to, which opponent you are playing against and maybe even the score or the amount of playing time left on the clock. For example, if there is not long left to play, and you're playing against a team that does not press, then it might make sense to go short and guarantee your team keeps possession.

The rule change has sparked a clear shift in tactics, as most goalkeepers now prefer to pass the ball **short** to a nearby teammate. This can be risky, as losing possession so close to goal can lead to conceding goals.

But there is also an upside. If your team is in possession and can pass the ball through your opponents, it can lead to a chance at the other end of the pitch. In fact, teams are more likely to have the ball in the opposition goal area within sixty seconds from a goal kick if that kick is taken short rather than long!

Since the rule change, the rate of successful passes, where the ball is safely received by a teammate from the goalkeeper, has risen. When records first began in 2004, the pass completion rate for goalkeepers was 43 per cent. In 2025, that figure went up to 69 per cent.

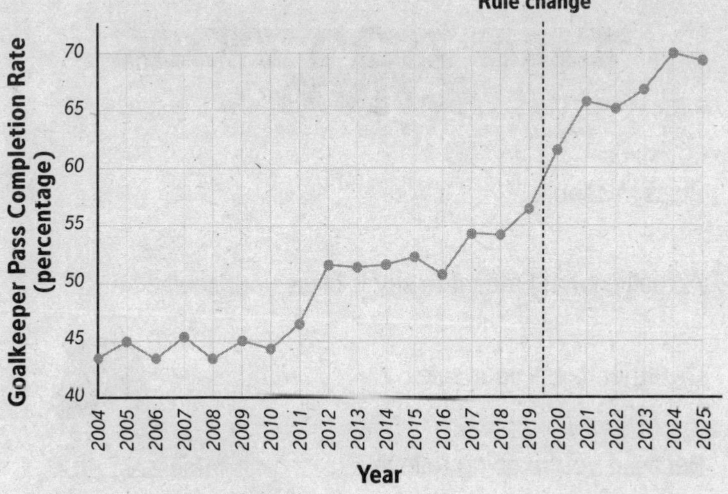

As the distance of the passes has shortened, so the pass completion rate has increased. It's easier to find your target with shorter passing. In the case of Chelsea in 2025, over 80 per cent of goal kicks stayed within their penalty area. Short kicks, long benefit!

Bless my soul!

Actually, what I meant to say is bless your soul!

Or rather, bless your sole.

Because you're going to love this new way of receiving a backpass when you are not under pressure. Just use . . . the sole of your foot.

Normally, players control the ball with their instep, which is the inner side of the foot. So if you have the ball on your left side, it's harder to pass it to the right. And if you have the ball on the right, it's harder to play to the left.

But this means that players coming to tackle you can predict where you will be passing, and adjust their angle to try to block that pass. Controlling the ball with the sole, or the studs of your boot, allows you to pass either left or right more easily. It will make it harder for your opponent to block off a pass. And it can even give you half a second of extra time because you don't have to look down for the ball – you know exactly where it is because you can feel it against the bottom of your foot, which you can't do when the ball is at your instep! Sole-crushing for the opposition.

When the opposition is slow to come forward and put the pressure on, you can use your sole to wait for the press as long as you want.

In one England youth match, defender Levi Colwill waited for over thirty seconds with the ball under his foot. That's a long time not to do anything with the ball in the middle of a match. People watching on television wondered if their screens had frozen! He was just waiting for the opposition to try to tackle him.

Waiting for a team to press is known as provoking, or baiting, the press. And using the sole of your boot to hold on to the ball is a very effective way to do this. All you need is studs on your boots – and patience. You'll find it's very good for the soul!

CATA DRIBBLE

Catalina Coll is a part of Spanish football history. She helped Spain win the 2023 World Cup after an outstanding performance in a 1–0 win over England in the final. Coll was twenty-two at the time, and it was only her fourth game playing for Spain!

Coll is a truly modern goalkeeper. She accepts that she is in the team to make great saves and to stop the ball going into the net. But she also wants to be known for how good she is with her outfield play and what she does with her passing and dribbling – she loves it when her teammates treat her like another outfield player.

'I'd rather be known as Cata Regate [*regate* is Spanish for dribble] because it's what defines me best,' she says.

Coll trains a lot with the ball at her feet. She is always practising how to pass through a high press – which is when opposition players swarm around you to try to win the ball. And all that practising pays off. She has a pass completion rate of over 94 per cent. (That means out of every hundred passes she's made, over ninety-four found a teammate.)

Coll has helped Barcelona Femení win three Champions Leagues and five Spanish league titles. In the 2023–24 season, the team won an extraordinary four trophies: the Champions League, the Spanish league, the Spanish Cup and the Spanish Super Cup. That was the season in which Barcelona Femení coach Jonatan Giráldez asked Coll to play like a third centre-back. Her starting position was high up the pitch, sometimes even close to the half-way line!

Coll is confident and a risk-taker. Playing that high up the pitch, she has to be!

What we learned in this chapter

Frans Hoek – Goalkeepers are part of the team and need to train with the team.

Ederson – Being good at passing is like giving the team an extra centre-back.

Eddy Treijtel – Look out for birds before taking a goal kick.

Alireza Beiranvand – Don't underestimate the power of throwing practice.

Cata Coll – Take risks and be confident in your abilities.

4
PENALTIES

Imagine you're a goalkeeper in a World Cup final and the referee has just awarded a penalty to the other team.

A penalty is awarded after a foul in the penalty area. It is a free shot on goal from twelve yards away, with just the goalkeeper to beat. It's a nerve-wracking moment for any goalkeeper. But if you think you're nervous, the person taking the penalty is going to be much, much more scared!

Players are expected to score a penalty. On average, a penalty is scored about 80 per cent of the time. That means out of a hundred penalties, eighty will be scored and twenty not scored. So the chances are, the penalty will go in. After all, if you're good enough at football to play for a club or even your country, you should be able to score from a free shot on goal. But many, including some of the best players in the world, don't score.

And NO player wants to be the one who misses.

Players who have missed an important* penalty

Lionel Messi (Argentina, Copa América 2016, Copa América 2024)
Kylian Mbappé (France, Euro 2020)
Bukayo Saka (England, Euro 2020)
Virgil van Dijk (Netherlands, 2022 World Cup)
Marta (Brazil, 2007 World Cup final)
Cristiano Ronaldo (Portugal, Euro 2024)
Lauren James (England, Euro 2025)

*in this case, important means for their national team at a major tournament

This is why the penalty kick is great for goalkeepers. If everyone expects the player to score, that means they do not expect the goalkeeper to save it. There's far less pressure on the goalkeeper. This is the one moment where they can be the hero – but not the villain! (Usually it's the other way around.)

It's certainly not impossible to save a penalty, though – whoever is taking it. And in this chapter, we will learn the techniques and tactics for stopping penalties from the best goalkeeper in the world. We will discover how the game Rock, Paper, Scissors might help you save a penalty. We will meet the showman who had a magical way of distracting opponents. And we will discover something new about butterflies, frogs and chaos!

But first, let's go to Northern Ireland in 1890 and meet the inventor of the penalty. He was, of course, a goalkeeper!

Did you know? One team refused to believe in penalties. Corinthians was an English amateur team that only played friendly matches, and their players believed that no one would deliberately foul an opponent. So when penalties first started being awarded in the 1890s, they would miss the target on purpose! One of the players ended up introducing football to Brazil and helped create one of Brazil's most popular and successful clubs today – Corinthians, named after his former team. And those Corinthians do score penalties!

SETTING THE STAGE

Willie McCrum played in goal for a team in Northern Ireland called Milford FC in 1890. After poor Willie let in sixty-two goals in just fourteen games, the team finished bottom of the league. Not good!

Willie hated the violent defending he saw in front of him. Some fouls were so vicious that players often ended up in hospital.

McCrum thought that punishing these fouls by giving the opposition a free shot on goal would encourage better behaviour on the pitch. So he wrote a proposal to the Irish Football Association to introduce the penalty kick. They passed it on to the International Football Association Board (known as IFAB), who made the rules of football then and still do.

When the English Football Association first heard of McCrum's idea, they disliked it. Like the Corinthians, they believed football was a game played by gentlemen who wouldn't deliberately foul anyone. Then they watched a controversial FA Cup match between Stoke City and Notts County. Stoke were losing when, in the last minute, they took a shot that looked to be heading in. That was until a Notts County defender punched the ball away off the goal line. No goal (and no penalty) was awarded. It was an outrage!

That incident persuaded the lawmakers to change their minds. In June 1891, the penalty was born. Back then, there were a few differences to the penalty as we know it now:

- The penalty could be taken anywhere along a twelve-yard line, not just on the penalty spot, which was added in 1902.
- It was also up to players to appeal for a penalty, whereas today they have to wait for the referee to award it.

McCrum wasn't just a goalkeeper; he was also an amateur actor and was used to having all eyes on him on the stage! In fact, it was suggested that he only invented the penalty so goalkeepers would have more attention on them. True or not, that's certainly what happened. Goalkeepers who save penalties always become the star of the show!

ZERO SUMS

Let's play a game of Rock, Paper, Scissors!

I pick paper. You pick scissors. You win! I lose.

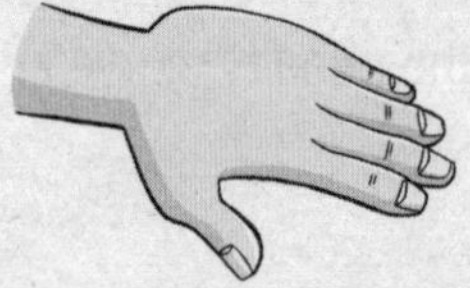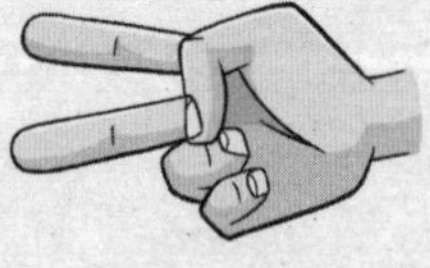

Now I pick rock. You pick scissors. I win! You lose! It's now 1–1.

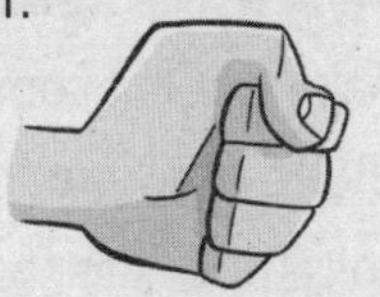 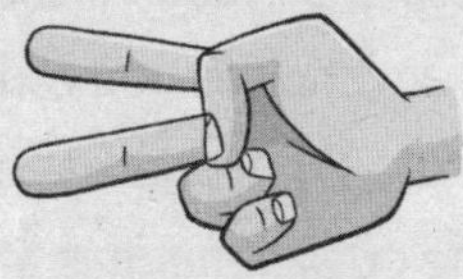

Deciding round: I go for rock again. This time, you go for paper. You win 2–1! I lose. Well done!

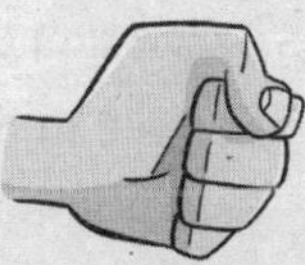 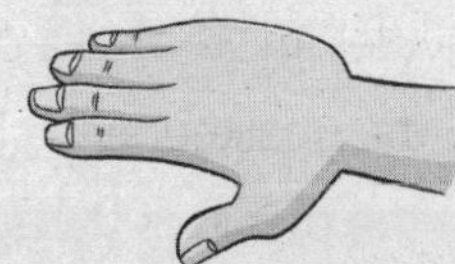

That was fun. We love this game because someone always wins. Which means someone else always loses. It's similar to tossing a coin and calling heads or tails. It can't be both! There's always one winner and one loser. The penalty kick is the same.

We call this type of duel a zero-sum game. That means someone has to win and someone has to lose: there is no scenario where both the goalkeeper and the kicker can be happy. It's called 'zero sum' because if you add up the wins and losses, they cancel out to zero.

Just as you can choose your options when you play Rock, Paper, Scissors, or you can choose between heads or tails, there are choices you can make when it comes to a penalty kick. The kicker has a choice of where to aim the ball. The goalkeeper has a choice of where to dive. Neither knows what the other one will do.

So how do they make these choices? Well, in a penalty shoot-out, the goalkeeper's choice of where to dive might depend on the previous shots taken or dive directions in the shoot-out so far.

A penalty shoot-out happens when a knockout game ends in a draw, usually after extra time. In the shoot-out, each team takes turns attempting five penalties each, and whoever scores the most penalties wins. If the score is still tied after five penalties each, the teams keep going until one team scores and the other misses.

Let's look at one of the most spectacular penalty shoot-outs in football history, when Barcelona played an all-Romanian team from that country's capital called Steaua Bucharest in the final of the 1986 European Cup (that's what the Champions League used to be called).

The game finished 0–0 after extra time and so went to a penalty shoot-out.

Steaua missed their first penalty. The Steaua goalkeeper Helmut Duckadam then had his first decision to make.

Decision 1

Duckadam: 'The kicker is right-footed. I think he will kick to his natural side, which is to my right.'
Decision: Duckadam dived to his right

Outcome: Duckadam was correct! Penalty save!

Steaua missed their next penalty too. Then it was time for Duckadam's second decision. This time, he put himself in the shoes of the Barcelona kicker, Spaniard Ángel Pedraza.

Decision 2

Duckadam: 'I dived to my right last time. The kicker will think I'm not going to do that again. So I'll dive to my right again.'

Decision: Duckadam dived to his right

Outcome: Duckadam was correct! Penalty save!

After two penalties each, the score in the shoot-out was, amazingly, 0–0. Steaua striker Marius Lăcătuş stepped forward next and finally scored to put his side 1–0 ahead. Up stepped Barcelona and former Spain forward Pichi Alonso, and Duckadam had another decision to make.

Decision 3

Duckadam: 'After going to the right twice, the kicker will definitely think I'm going to change sides. So I'll dive to my right again.'

Decision: Duckadam dived to his right

Outcome: Duckadam was correct! Another penalty save!

Steaua then scored their next penalty, and were 2–0 ahead when Spaniard Marcos Alonso took the ball for Barcelona. Once again, Duckadam wondered what his opponent might be thinking.

Decision 4

Duckadam: 'I've dived to the right three times in a row.
The kicker will think that's the only place I ever dive.
So this time, I'm going to change sides and dive to
my left.'
Decision: Duckadam dived to his left
Outcome: Duckadam was correct! A fourth penalty save!
Historic!

STEAUA BUCHAREST 2 BARCELONA 0

No goalkeeper since has ever saved four shoot-
out penalties in a row in such an important game.
Duckadam called himself a penalty specialist and said
it was because he could always get into the minds of
his opponents. He was a really good poker player, too,
because he could tell whether an opponent was bluffing
(pretending to have good cards) or not.

Because of a mysterious injury to his arm, this was the
last serious football match that Duckadam ever played.
Talk about finishing on a high!

When Duckadam played card games with his friends, he would observe them carefully, looking out for certain behaviours that gave away clues about whether they were bluffing. Maybe one player would swallow loudly or look to the left; another might blink rapidly or bite their upper lip. Every action reveals a clue!

The role of the goalkeeper during a penalty is to act as a detective and spot any clues that might reveal where the kicker will aim for.

Here are some clues to look out for:

Kicker gaze

It's likely that at some point between putting the ball on the spot and taking the penalty, the kicker will look at the area of the goal where they want to shoot. It could be after they place the ball down or before they start their run-up. So always keep your eyes peeled to see where the kicker is looking!

Angle of run-up

- If the angle of the kicker's run-up is very straight, expect a shot to the kicker's natural side. (Kicking to the natural side means kicking across the body, so a right-footer would naturally kick to their left and a left-footer to their right.)

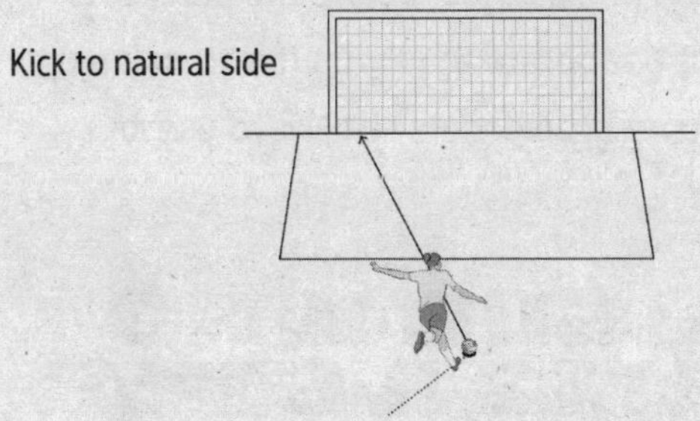

- If the angle of the kicker's run-up is very wide, expect a shot to the kicker's non-natural side.

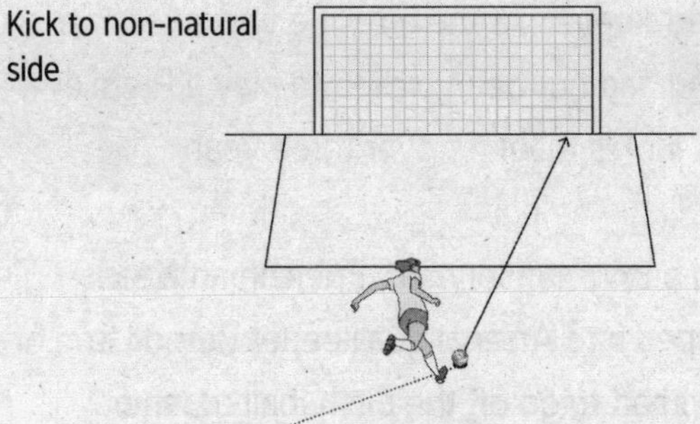

- If the angle of the kicker's run-up is somewhere in between, then it's hard to tell!

Standing foot

The direction of the kicker's standing foot – that is, the foot that is not kicking the ball – will often point to where the penalty will be going. So if the toe of the standing foot is facing to the goalkeeper's left, the ball is likely to be going there too. The problem is that you can only see this very late in the process, just before the penalty is struck, so it might be too late to rely on this to make up your mind. But some goalkeepers still like to use it!

THE SUB WHO BECAME A STAR

Emiliano Martínez was sitting on the Arsenal substitutes' bench one sunny day in June 2020 when his life changed forever. At the time, he was a reserve goalkeeper and had not been picked to play a Premier League game for his team for over three years.

That was until a Brighton forward, Frenchman Neal Maupay, bumped into Arsenal goalkeeper Bernd Leno of Germany, who had to go off the pitch injured, and

Martínez was called up to play the rest of the game. This was his chance. Martínez was back on the pitch!

What happened next was incredible.

- Martínez plays well for Arsenal and wins the FA Cup that season.
- He signs for Aston Villa later that summer and plays the full 2020–21 season for them.
- Martínez is called up to play for Argentina's national team in June 2021.
- Just weeks later, he helps Argentina win the Copa América, the continental tournament for South America, for the first time in twenty-eight years.
- Martínez plays for Argentina in the 2022 World Cup, where they win two penalty shoot-outs and the final to be crowned world champions.
- He is named the best goalkeeper in the world in 2022.
- In 2024, Martínez is named the best goalkeeper in the world . . . again!

In a short space of time, Martínez had transformed from a forgotten substitute into a global superstar.

But would any of this have happened without Neal
Maupay fouling Leno on that fateful day in 2020?
We will never know.

A small event can have huge consequences. For example,
imagine your parents first met at a coffee shop. Now imagine
what could have happened if your mum, for example,
hadn't wanted a coffee that day or your dad had turned
up five minutes later? Would they still have met? The idea
that a small thing like buying a coffee can have long-lasting
consequences, like falling in love and having a
family, is called the butterfly effect. The
name comes from the idea that
something as small as a
butterfly flapping its
wings in Brazil might
end up changing
the weather in America.
Or, in football terms, a
Brighton striker fouling a German
goalkeeper can end up helping
Argentina win the World Cup!

The butterfly effect is a part of chaos theory. And if there's
one thing that Emiliano Martínez believes in, it's chaos!

SHOOT-OUT SUPERPOWER

Martínez can stop penalties in a shoot-out like no
one else.

Before the 2022 World Cup, these were the rules for the
goalkeeper during a shoot-out:

The goalkeeper:
- must face the ball
- must be on the goal line and between
  the goalposts
- can move along the goal line and/or
  jump up and down, as long as at least
  part of each foot is on or above the
  line, until the ball is kicked
- must have at least part of one foot
  touching, in line with, or behind the
  goal line when the ball is kicked

His Argentina teammate Lionel Messi once gave Martínez
a useful piece of advice. Messi said that strikers don't like
it when goalkeepers move around on the goal line. It's
distracting and much harder to pick a spot and aim for it
if the goalkeeper is always moving. Not everyone can get

tips from one of the best players of all time, so when you do, you listen!

Since then, Martínez always tries to be disruptive. He says, 'Creating pressure on the opponent gives me confidence!'

So what are some of his disruptive tactics?

Verbal disruption – talking to the referee or kicker to distract the taker

Kick delay – taking ages to get ready, so the kicker has to wait around. Delay tactics include chatting to the kicker, walking very slowly to the goal line or taking a drink of water at the last minute to slow things down. This can frustrate the kicker and make them feel angry and impatient ahead of their important penalty – or give them more time to worry about it!

Ball possession – holding on to the ball. This can disrupt the kicker's routine, slow them down or even force them to walk to a different part of the pitch to get the ball.

Visual distraction – dancing, jumping or moving in a way that surprises the kicker

Penalty-spot confrontation – before the kick is taken, approaching the kicker and chatting to them near the penalty spot. This is intimidating, as the goalkeeper should be on the goal line, while the penalty spot is for the kicker.

Fan control – gesturing at fans to wind them up and distract the kicker

As he puts it: 'I create chaos.'

Now let's look at when Martínez has used these tactics during a penalty shoot-out.

SHOOT-OUT 1: ARSENAL 5 LIVERPOOL 4
Community Shield, August 2020

As the shoot-out goes on, Martínez becomes more talkative towards his opponents, winking, chatting and trying to put them off. He knows that making kickers wait improves his chances of success, and it works: Liverpool's third kicker hits the crossbar.

Tactics: Verbal disruption, kick delay

Penalty stops: 1/5

Outcome: Victory number one!

SHOOT-OUT 2: ARGENTINA 3 COLOMBIA 2
Copa América semi-final, July 2021

During one player's run-up, Martínez says: 'I'm eating you up, brother!' He goes on to save that penalty. To the next player he shouts: 'You're laughing but you're nervous. I know where you'll shoot and save it.' He saves it. Martínez waits for the fourth kicker at the penalty spot before chatting at him. He then saves Colombia's last penalty, and Argentina make it to the final.

Tactics: Verbal disruption, kick delay, penalty-spot confrontation

Penalty stops: 3/5

Outcome: Success number two!

SHOOT-OUT 3: ARGENTINA 4 NETHERLANDS 3
World Cup quarter-final, December 2022

After Martínez saves the first penalty, he does a cheeky dance to celebrate. Before the second penalty, he offers to give the ball to the kicker, but then deliberately drops the ball a few metres away. That winds up the player, who misses his penalty as Martínez saves it. The Argentinian does another dance to celebrate. Before the fourth kick, Martínez kicks the ball forty metres away and kisses both goalposts to make the kicker wait even longer. The Dutch player scores, but Martínez's distraction tactics are clear.

Tactics: Verbal disruption, kick delay, ball possession, visual distraction

Penalty stops: 2/5

Outcome: Triumph number three!

SHOOT-OUT 4: ARGENTINA 4 FRANCE 2

World Cup final, December 2022

This is the biggest moment of Martínez's career. Before France's second penalty, he meets the kicker at the spot and chats to him. He then delays the kick further by asking the referee to check if the ball is on the spot. 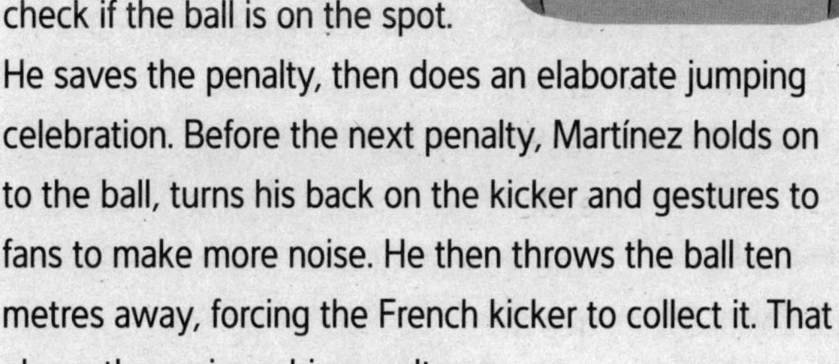
He saves the penalty, then does an elaborate jumping celebration. Before the next penalty, Martínez holds on to the ball, turns his back on the kicker and gestures to fans to make more noise. He then throws the ball ten metres away, forcing the French kicker to collect it. That player then misses his penalty.

Tactics: Verbal disruption, kick delay, ball possession, visual distraction, penalty-spot confrontation, fan control

Penalty stops: 2/4

Outcome: Glory number four!

Martínez's chaos worked. But the people who make football's rules did not like these tactics of delay and distraction. In July 2023, they added one more rule for goalkeepers to the Laws of the Game:

> The goalkeeper must not behave in a way that unfairly distracts the kicker, e.g., delay the taking of the kick or touch the goalposts, crossbar or net.

Did this new rule put an end to Martínez's chaos? What do you think? Of course not!

The phrase 'unfairly distract' is hard to define exactly, and still does not prevent goalkeepers from taking up unusual positions on the goal line, talking to opponents or finding new ways to delay the penalty kick.

IMPORTANT NOTE: I expect that Martínez's trickery would not be allowed in your school football matches, so I am certainly not recommending copying his tactics. I don't want to get in trouble with your teachers!

After the new rule came in, Martínez took part in more penalty shoot-outs. You'll never guess what happened . . .

SHOOT-OUT 5: ASTON VILLA 4 LILLE 3
UEFA Europa Conference League quarter-final, May 2024
Before the first penalty, Martínez goes to the penalty spot to stare at the kicker, picks up the ball and throws it away! He then saves the penalty, before turning to the crowd and putting a finger to his lips in a 'shush' gesture. That infuriates the fans! He continues to wind them up, and is shown a yellow card. This still doesn't stop him from saving the fifth kick to complete an amazing record in shoot-outs. Played five, won five!
Tactics: Kick delay, ball possession, visual distraction, fan control
Penalty stops: 2/4
Outcome: Victory again – number five!

SHOOT-OUT 6: ARGENTINA 4 ECUADOR 2
Copa América quarter-final, July 2024

Once again, Martínez doesn't technically break the new
rule, but still causes disruption. He jumps on his goal line,
arms raised, wiggling his hips before leaping to his left
to save the first penalty. He then turns to the Argentina
fans behind the goal and encourages them to show their
support. After his second penalty save, an impressive
dive to his right, he faces his fans again and, knees bent,
dances in front of them. Before the next penalty, he
stands to one side of the goal, attempting to trick the
penalty-taker into aiming for a certain spot. This time,
the kicker gets it right – but Martínez is always trying.
And with those two saves, it was his fourth straight
shoot-out success in Argentina colours.

Tactics: Ball possession, visual distraction, fan control

Penalty stops: 2/5

Outcome: Continues the 100 per cent record –
six out of six!

MARVELLOUS MARTÍNEZ

Remember I told you that a penalty is scored about 80 per cent of the time? So, in a shoot-out of five penalties per team, that means on average each team will score four and miss one.

This means the average saving rate for goalkeepers in penalty shoot-outs is around 20 per cent.

Let's look at the numbers:

All goalkeepers, on average:

Total pens faced	Scored	Saved	Saving rate
100	78	22	22 per cent

Martínez's saving rate in penalty shoot-outs for Argentina:

Total pens faced	Scored	Saved	Saving rate
24	12	12	50 per cent

Martínez is a true penalty great!

DISTRACTION TECHNIQUES

Martínez isn't the only goalkeeper who likes to use distraction techniques. Some goalkeepers will do anything to put off an opponent during a penalty. Here are some examples – although I don't recommend you try these yourself!

Goalkeeper	Team	Tactic	Outcome
Jerzy Dudek	Liverpool	Waved his arms and pointed at areas of the goal	Saved two penalties, won 2005 Champions League final
He said: 'My teammate Jamie Carragher shouted at me, "Try to do something to put them off. Distract them!"'			
Mickaël Landreau	Nantes	Stood next to one post	Saved the penalty, Ronaldinho hit the ball straight at him
He said: 'They called me a genius but you just have to take some chances.'			
Andrew Redmayne	Australia	Danced on goal line	Saved two penalties, reached 2022 World Cup
He said: 'If I can make a clown of myself to help my team win, I'm happy to do that.'			
Stephanie Labbé	Canada	Smiled at her opponents	Saved the penalty, won 2020 Olympic gold medal
She said: 'I know how much body language can have an effect on people.'			

Mickaël Landreau

Andrew Redmayne

Stephanie Labbé

Did you know? Germany goalkeeper Ann-Katrin Berger has a different technique when it comes to penalties. She waits on the centre of the goal line with her hands behind her back, looking like she doesn't have a care in the world. She prepares before the game, writing on her water bottle who she thinks will take penalties and where they will probably aim their kicks. In between each penalty, she drinks some water and checks her notes. Normally it works! This tactic has helped her win penalty shoot-outs for Chelsea in the Champions League and Germany in the Olympics and at Euro 2025. In the latter two tournaments, she even scored penalties as well!

MEET THE MAGICIAN

In the middle of a penalty shoot-out in a 2023 competition called the Leagues Cup, Argentine goalkeeper Nahuel Guzmán pointed at the referee and asked for a moment. He was clutching his stomach and bent over as though he was in pain. Guzmán was playing for Mexican team Tigres, and his team were currently ahead 4–3 in the shoot-out against Vancouver Whitecaps.

Whitecaps and Serbia defender Ranko Veselinović was waiting to take his penalty. He watched on in shock as Guzmán bent over. The goalkeeper then stood up and put his gloves to his mouth. He opened his mouth, stuck in a glove and pulled out some pink string. Actually, a lot of pink string. Guzmán had twenty metres of the stuff stuck in his mouth, and he was pulling it out like a magician doing a party trick. That pink string just kept coming!

It was not the first time Guzmán had tried something like this. In the same penalty shoot-out, just two kicks earlier, he had distracted Mexican midfielder Sebastián Córdova with a mime routine. With eyes wide, he put his hands in front of his face, and silently acted as though he was pushing against an invisible wall. On this occasion, Córdova was unaffected by the mime act and scored his penalty.

You could not say the same for Veselinović. With a pile of pink string lying at the foot of one post, and Guzmán booked for delaying the kick, he struck his penalty to the right . . . and straight into Guzmán's arms. Uruguayan Fernando Gorriarán scored the next penalty for Tigres, who won the game.

But what was Guzmán playing at? He later revealed that the ideas came from some friends who work as clowns. They thought it would be a funny way to protest against the rule changes around goalkeeper distraction tactics, which are not violent or aggressive.

'There are ways to intervene creatively and in a fun way too,' he said.

Guzmán remains a showman: one week later, in the next round of the competition, he prepared for a penalty by pretending to tiptoe across his goal line like a trapeze artist hundreds of feet off the ground. Did it work? Not this time! But there might be a next time, and who knows what circus act Guzmán will pull out next!

TAKE NOTE!

As we are learning, penalties are a lot about skill and technique, but tricks, tactics and mind games often come into play too! And, sometimes, just pretending that you know more than your opponent can be enough to gain an advantage. That worked for Germany goalkeeper Jens Lehmann in the 2006 World Cup quarter-final against Argentina. The game finished 1–1 and went to a penalty shoot-out.

Before Argentina's first penalty, Lehmann pulled out a piece of paper from inside his sock that was tucked behind his shin-pad. On it was a list of seven Argentine players and their preferred penalty directions. Germany's goalkeeping coach Andreas Köpke had written out the list and given it to Lehmann before the game, just in case. Here's some of what was originally written on the paper:

Germany took the first penalty and scored. 1–0.

Lehmann looked at the piece of paper before Julio
Cruz took Argentina's first penalty. His name was not
there! Lehmann took a guess and dived the correct way
– to his right. The shot went into the top corner, and
Argentina scored. 1–1.

Germany scored again. 2–1.

Next came Ayala: the note said he would kick to the
goalkeeper's left. So Lehmann dived to his left . . . and
saved it! Still 2–1.

Germany scored again. 3–1.

Now Rodríguez stepped up. The note said he would
kick to the goalkeeper's right. So Lehmann dived in that
direction . . . and it went just under him! 3–2.

Germany scored again. 4–2.

Next up for Argentina was Cambiasso. Lehmann took out the piece of paper and looked at it long and hard. There was no Cambiasso on it. He had no idea what to do! But then again . . . nor did Cambiasso. The Argentine thought that Lehmann knew what he was going to do, though. And that thought was enough to spook him. He kicked to his right, and Lehmann made the save.

Final score in the shoot-out: Germany 4 Argentina 2.

There was a twist. After the game, Lehmann revealed that Köpke had written out the list of players in pencil. After over two hours stuck in his sock, the piece of paper was covered in sweat, and the writing had completely rubbed out. Lehmann was looking at the paper, but couldn't read any of it!

It turned out that just making his opponents believe that he knew what they were going to do was enough to put them off.

He made two great saves in the shoot-out – just imagine if he'd actually been able to read the notes!

What we learned in this chapter

Willie McCrum – The penalty kick is the perfect stage for the goalkeeper to stand out and show off their skills.

Helmut Duckadam – Read your opponent's body language to get into their minds and guess their next move.

Emiliano Martínez – Causing chaos (within the rules) can stop penalties.

Ann-Katrin Berger – Feeling prepared can fill you with confidence.

Nahuel Guzmán – There's always time for some magic on the pitch – as long as it doesn't get you in trouble!

5
COMMUNICATION

Wait! Go! Stay! Move! Behind! Left! Time!

In this chapter, we are going to look up, look out and hit the heights. We are going to discover why goalkeepers are like air-traffic controllers.

Air-traffic controllers help aeroplanes fly safely by telling pilots when they can take off and land. They use radar screens so they can see where all the planes are and make sure there is enough space between the planes so they don't bump into each other. They talk to the pilots through a radio and communicate using specific phrases that give clear information and instructions.

Goalkeepers are very similar. As the player who is usually closest to the goal line, they can see everything that's happening on the pitch in a way that defenders cannot.

- If an opponent is making a run at the far post, the goalkeeper can see it.
- If a midfielder is making a late run into the box, the goalkeeper can see it.
- If a striker is looking to run past a defender, the goalkeeper can see it.

Because of this advantage, goalkeepers manage the space around the goal. They can organize the defence, directing them to mark opponents, block shots, anticipate passes and prevent chances being created.

The best way to do that? Just like air-traffic controllers, who are also working under high pressure and having to react quickly, it's by talking, using clear and precise communication. And sometimes, if they really have to, SHOUTING!

Goalkeepers who would be good air-traffic controllers:

Hann-air Hampton

Air-on Ramsdale

Giorgi Mam-air-dashvili

In this chapter, we will learn the best phrases that goalkeepers can use to communicate clearly to their defenders, and the best tone of voice to get the message across. We will also discover a new language for goalkeepers – which doesn't involve any words at all. But first, we're going to meet the multilingual goalkeeper who never stopped chatting during matches, and the one who forgot to talk to his teammates entirely!

BACK IN THE MISTS OF TIME

Englishman Sam Bartram was a goalkeeper for Charlton Athletic. He was popular and loyal. He ended up playing over 600 times for Charlton, although he is remembered for one match in particular, which was played on Christmas Day in 1937.

The game was at Chelsea's Stamford Bridge stadium. It was a cold and misty day, and as the match went on, a thick fog rolled across the pitch.

Bartram tried to focus on what was ahead of him. He couldn't see his teammates at all in the fog, so he assumed they were at the other end of the pitch, pushing to score a goal. And as he couldn't see anyone dropping back for the kick-off, he assumed they hadn't scored yet.

So he waited. He stamped his feet to keep warm and moved forward to the edge of his penalty area, ready to go when he was needed. As time passed, he was feeling very proud of his teammates. They were clearly spending a lot of time putting pressure on the Chelsea goal, as he hadn't seen them for ages!

After a while, a figure emerged from the fog, walking towards Bartram. It was a policeman, and he stared at the goalkeeper incredulously.

'What on earth are you doing here?' the policeman asked. 'The game was stopped fifteen minutes ago. The pitch is completely empty.'

The match had been called off because of the fog. But no one had thought to tell poor Bartram! Not the referee, the twenty-one other players, the two managers or anyone in the crowd of around 40,000 people. When Bartram eventually made it back to the dressing room, his teammates, who were all showered and ready to go home, thought it was hilarious.

And while the idea of one player dutifully guarding his goal on an empty pitch does sound funny, there is also something a little sad about Bartram's situation. No one considered the goalkeeper. He was not really part of the team – he was more of an outsider, someone who could be easily forgotten about.

That's no longer the case now. But if there had been better communication between Bartram and his teammates, he might have escaped his fifteen-minute foggy fate.

ČECH MATES

A Spaniard, a Frenchman and a German walked on to the pitch. This is not the start of a bad joke – it's just a regular event in the Premier League!

They were all playing in defence, and behind them was a goalkeeper who was Czech. Not only was he Czech, his name was also Čech (which is pronounced the same)! Petr Čech was a brilliant goalkeeper, an international player with over 100 appearances for Czechia, and a Champions League winner with Chelsea.

When Čech signed for Arsenal in 2015, he played behind two Spanish full-backs (Nacho Monreal and Héctor Bellerín), a French centre-back (Laurent Koscielny) and a German centre-back (Per Mertesacker).

Čech was a smart guy and a brilliant communicator. He understood that playing in defence is demanding and stressful. He also realized that it might help his defenders if he gave them one less thing to think about on the pitch. With players having only milliseconds to process information and make decisions, he came up with a solution: to talk to the players in their own language!

He spoke to Monreal and Bellerín in Spanish. *Sí!*
He spoke to Koscielny in French. *Oui!*
And he spoke to Mertesacker in . . . English!
(The German player was fluent in English and
said he was fine with it.) Yes!

'If you are not familiar with all the football terms, in the heat of the moment and under pressure, you might not understand what your teammate is asking for,' Čech explained. 'For some people, it's easier when they hear it in their native language. It means they don't have to translate anything.'

Čech was a walking language dictionary, and it was so helpful in improving the communication between him and his teammates. And most important of all? He could say 'Mine!' in multiple languages! *Mío! Le mien! Meins!*

Did you know? Petr Čech holds the record for the most clean sheets in the Premier League: he achieved 202 clean sheets in 443 Premier League appearances playing for Chelsea (333 games) and Arsenal (110 games). In his first season at Chelsea, he broke the record for clean sheets in one season (twenty-four in thirty-five games) and went more than 1,000 minutes (over eleven games) without conceding a goal. He was also incredibly brave: he once fractured his skull when an opponent's knee struck his head as he was diving for the ball. He spent three months recovering and then played for the rest of his career – another thirteen years – wearing a foam head guard to protect his skull. After retiring, he returned to his favourite childhood sport, ice hockey, and spent the next few years playing as, you guessed It, a goalie!

SAY WHAT?

It's time for an impression!

Think of your strictest teacher. And your naughtiest classmate.

Now, remember a time that the teacher caught the naughty pupil misbehaving and shouted at them. What did the teacher say?

And more importantly, what tone of voice did they use?

It was probably loud, clear and firm (with some extra grumpiness, too, I'd imagine).

Goalkeepers need to use a similar tone. When the ball is flying around the goal area or the opposition are about to take a set piece, goalkeepers don't have much time to say what they need to say.

So, as a keeper, you need to impersonate your strictest teacher. Be loud, to the point and speak with authority. Use short words or phrases. Be specific. And be strict! It doesn't mean you're cross with your teammates – or that you'll put them in detention!

A goalkeeper who can communicate well will improve teamwork, performance and confidence among the defence. They will keep their teammates alert and focused, and create a supportive environment for everyone.

Here are some words – and their definitions – that every goalkeeper can use on the pitch. But make sure your teammates know what these words mean if you plan to use them in a game!

The Goalkeeper's Dictionary

BACK!

Definition: I am free, and you can pass the
ball back to me.

Use when: You want to give your defender the
option to pass to you.

CLEAR!

Definition: Get rid of the ball as quickly as possible.

Use when: You want your defender to get the ball
away from the goal area quickly. Your teammates
can't always see what's behind or around them,
but your shout can warn them if they need to get
moving.

KEEPER!

Definition: I'm coming for the ball, so get
out of the way.

Use when: You need space to claim the ball. This is
most often used when it's a high ball, and people
are crowding around to get to it.

MAN ON!

Definition: Pass the ball quickly or shield it, because an opponent is about to challenge you.

Use when: A teammate is being pressed by an opponent.

NEAR (OR FAR) POST!

Definition: Stand next to one of the goalposts to help protect that area of the goal.

Use when: Preparing for a set piece, when you want a specific corner of the goal covered.

PUSH UP!

Definition: Move away from the goal and up the pitch.

Use when: You want your defenders positioned higher up the pitch to launch a quick attack, or to catch an opponent offside.

TIME!

Definition: Take a second! You have more time than you think to make your next decision.

Use when: Your defender is not under pressure from any opponents and doesn't need to rush to clear the ball.

MARY, MARY, VERY SCARY*

(*IF YOU'RE A STRIKER)

Ex-England goalkeeper Mary Earps fell in love with goalkeeping in her very first match. She was ten years old, playing for West Bridgford Colts girls. Everyone had to take a turn in goal, and when Earps went in, she was reluctant at first. She spent a lot of the time cartwheeling between the posts until she had to face a penalty. And she saved it! That was enough for her. She knew she'd be a goalkeeper for life.

Even at that age, Earps was never afraid to shout at her defenders and warn them where their opponents were. That marked her out as a bit different. A lot of young goalkeepers are nervous or embarrassed to tell their defenders what to do. Don't be – it's a really important and useful skill.

Earps constantly talks to her teammates during a match, whether it's asking a player to slightly adjust their position or letting someone know there's an opponent at their shoulder. This chatter is always with one aim: to make the game easier for her teammates. She has a view of the pitch that they don't, and any extra information she can give might save some seconds or stop a chance.

'All I'm trying to do is help the team,' she says.

And that's exactly what she did on one sunny August evening in Australia in 2023. Earps was standing behind her goal line, waiting to face a penalty. It was the World Cup final, and as well as 75,000 fans watching in the stadium, there were over 65 million viewers watching on television across the world. That's a lot of eyeballs on Mary!

Earps was waiting for Spain striker Jenni Hermoso to take
the penalty. After a short run-up and a powerful strike
to the right side of the goal, Earps exploded off her line,
lunging forwards and at full stretch to her left. She gathered
the ball in her arms. It was an amazing save, and Earps was
named the best goalkeeper of the World Cup.

This wasn't her first award, though. In 2022, she won FIFA's
award for best goalkeeper of the year. She gave a powerful
speech, which ended with the inspiring words: 'There's only
one of you in the world, and that's more than good enough.
Be unapologetically yourself.' Yes, Mary!

Earps realizes the power of her words on and off the pitch. Before the 2023 World Cup, she publicly criticized the kit manufacturing company, who were selling the Lionesses' shirts but hadn't made it possible for fans to buy her goalkeeper shirt. She used her voice to speak out about this, and it worked. The manufacturer soon released 'Earps' goalkeeper shirts and they sold out in record time. No surprise!

'Goalkeeping is cool,' says Earps, 'and goalkeepers deserve to be treated the way you treat strikers.'

Even as a child, Earps was confident in speaking up and saying what she thinks. The sign of a great goalkeeper!

But words are not the only way to communicate and to inspire others.

WHO NEEDS WORDS?

Did you know that scientists believe that more than half of what we say doesn't come out of our mouths? Body language is a way of communicating without using words. We can use our posture, gestures, eye contact and facial expressions to show how we are feeling and what we're thinking.

Here's an example for you. Let's say you ask your friend how they are. 'I'm fine,' they say. But you can see they are looking down at their feet, have a frown on their forehead, their shoulders are slumped, and they have tears in their eyes. They may have said they are fine, but their body language is telling a different story: that they are sad or upset.

On the football pitch, using your body language can be a powerful weapon. The player who looks sharp, confident, lively and ready to go is giving off better signals than a teammate who is slouching, moving slowly and looks like they have no energy.

Coaches often ask players to use their body language to present themselves as focused, enthusiastic and ready to win. For all players, but especially for a goalkeeper, this can be a superpower. If you stand tall and put your arms out wide, you will look big and confident. You will feel big and confident. And just as importantly, your opponents will think you are big and confident too. That will make them more nervous against you!

Pep Guardiola, one of the most successful coaches of all time, says, 'You cannot play well when the body language is not correct.'

Body language is an important way of communicating with your teammates. Here are just some ways that goalkeepers can communicate without words but still send a strong message:

These are all signs to encourage and support your teammates. They send the messages 'I appreciate you' and 'together we can do this'.

Here's an example. Let's say your team has conceded a goal because your teammate made a mistake. They look

upset. You are the player nearest to them.
What do you do?

Option One: You stand right next to your teammate and point your finger at them. You shout, 'Why did you do that, you silly doughnut? Your mistake has cost the whole team. I'm so angry right now!'

Option Two: You give your teammate a high five and a hug. You calmly say, 'Don't worry about it. We all make mistakes; it's totally normal. Let's carry on and try to score the next goal.'

Which option would you choose?

Option two is a much better choice, of course! And it's far more likely to result in your team being successful during the rest of the match. No one plays well if they are worried about being shouted at.

Your reaction can influence not just a teammate who made a mistake, but the whole team. Staying calm and encouraging teammates sends a positive message to everyone.

EXPRESS YOURSELF DRILL

1. Write down ten emotions on ten pieces of paper and fold them up. The emotions could be: angry, anxious, calm, confident, excited, focused, joyful, lonely, proud, upset.

2. Place the pieces of paper in a bowl.

3. Stand opposite a friend and take out one piece of paper.

4. Act out that emotion using only your body and facial expressions – no words allowed – and get your friend to guess the emotion.

5. Now it's your friend's turn to act and you to guess.

6. Keep going until you've acted out all the emotions.

From a tactical point of view, using body language is also a great way of telling your teammates what to do and who to look out for without your opponent hearing. You can let your defender know that they need to keep an eye on an opponent by pointing an arm over here or nodding your head over there.

Through communication, with and without words, the best goalkeepers are leaders on the pitch! So the next time you're in goal, remember that your body language is just as important as the words you use.

BODY LANGUAGE DRILL

1. Watch a top goalkeeper during a match.

2. Look out for how they use their bodies to lead without words.

3. Practise these on a friend or family member. Try to communicate with them through body language alone and see if they understand.

BODY LANGUAGE TIPS

- Always stand as tall as you can – no slouching!

- Don't be afraid to wave your arms or point fingers, as long as it's clear what you are trying to say.

- Use eye contact with your teammates as much as possible so they know exactly who you're communicating with.

- After conceding a goal, clap your hands or console and support anyone who looks upset – we all make mistakes!

What we learned in this chapter

Sam Bartram –   Check the weather report before you play!

Petr Čech –   Communicate in a clear way that your teammates will understand.

Mary Earps –   Be confident when telling your defenders what to do.

Pep Guardiola –   Good body language will help you play better.

Mary Earps (again) – Be unapologetically yourself.

6

KIT

Do you want to be a hero?

Or are you ready to be a superhero?

Don't worry – you're playing in the right position for it!

French goalkeeper Jérémie Janot was more than ready. He played over 400 games for French top division team Saint-Étienne, and he was allowed to design his own kit. To celebrate one of his favourite ever characters, he took to the pitch wearing blue shorts and a red-and-blue top . . .

The top had a spider-web design on it, and his style choice was confirmed when the team lined up for its pre-match photo. As the players stood in two lines for the official picture, Janot pulled out a Spider-Man mask and put it on to complete the look.

Saint-Étienne had Spider-Man in goal!

He played like Spider-Man too.

Speed – extraordinary!
Reflexes – superb!
Agility – amazing!
Invincibility – yes, yes, yes!

Janot took off his mask during the match – but his
Spider-Man abilities didn't go away. His performance
was outstanding, and Saint-Étienne won 2–0. Once
again, Spider-Man had saved the day!

While most goalkeepers don't dress up as superheroes on the pitch, their kits have come a long way since the early days of football.

Before 1909, goalkeepers wore the same kit as the rest of the team. The only way to tell them apart was that some wore a flat cap. The rules then changed so goalkeepers had to wear a different colour long-sleeved shirt to their teammates – but only if it was red, white or blue! This was so referees could clearly see which player was the goalkeeper and, therefore, who was allowed to handle the ball. In 1912, green was added to the approved list of colours, and most goalkeepers wore a thick woollen green shirt.

In this chapter, we will explore how goalkeeper fashion has changed over the years and learn how your kit can improve your performance.

We will explain the science behind goalkeeper gloves, help you choose the ideal gloves and give you tips on how to look after your gloves to make them last as long as possible.

We will also meet the goalkeeper who played in a bedsheet (awkward!) and the one who showered in his gloves (even more awkward!).

Are you ready for the catwalk? Best foot – and hand – forward!

GLOVELY JUBBLY

Let's start with a question.

What do you wear to protect your hands if you are:

- a firefighter?
- skiing?
- a surgeon performing an operation?
- a gardener cutting down brambles?
- a goalkeeper, and players are kicking a ball really hard in your direction?

Have you worked out the answer to all of these?
It's ... GLOVES!

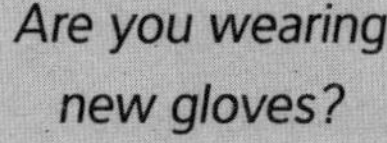

Yes, which on one hand
is great, but on the other
hand it's just not right.

Football came late to the glove party. A few goalkeepers were seen wearing gloves in the early 1900s – for example, Wales goalkeeper Leigh Roose was pictured in 1909 wearing woollen mittens. But it was only in 1945, when an Argentine goalkeeper called Amadeo Carrizo regularly wore cotton gloves in goal, that the trend really took off. News of his outfit spread to Europe, where it was copied, and gloves soon became seen as an important item for all goalkeepers to wear.

Newcastle United's English goalkeeper Jack Fairbrother once lost his gloves before a match. He asked a policeman who was patrolling the area behind his goal if he could borrow his.

'If they are good enough to stop traffic, they are good enough to stop goals,' he said.

He was right: Fairbrother went on to regularly wear police gloves in goal, including when Newcastle beat Blackpool 2–0 to win the 1951 FA Cup final.

England goalkeeper Gordon Banks was wearing what looked like gardening gloves when he made the Save of the Century at the 1970 World Cup (see page 68).

When Banks was playing football, the gloves were very different to the specialist goalkeeper gloves that we have now. They used to be made from cotton or wool, which got wet in the rain, making it hard to catch the ball. Now the main materials used for goalkeeper gloves are **latex** and **foam**.

Latex is a natural material that comes from rubber trees and is known for being sticky. It is used on the palm and fingers of the glove to help goalkeepers catch and hold the ball.

Beneath the latex is a soft layer of flexible foam, which adds padding. This makes the gloves comfortable and helps cushion the blow of a powerful strike.

The latex and foam give goalkeepers the three things that they need more than anything:

1. Comfort: Who wants to be uncomfortable doing their job? Not me, not you – and not goalkeepers! Just as boots should feel comfortable to wear, so should gloves. That means they need to be flexible, made with soft materials and breathable so your hands don't get too sweaty!

2. Grip: Grip is the act of holding on to something. If the gloves can't keep hold of the ball, it's a problem. The latex on the gloves stops them from being slippery. It allows the goalkeeper to make saves and to catch, punch and deflect the ball with greater accuracy.

3. Durability: Durability means lasting a long time without getting damaged – which is just what you want from your gloves. Goalkeeper gloves need to survive through dives, collisions and regular impact from the ball, without losing their ability to do their job! While the sturdy materials now used for gloves can help with durability, the palms are still delicate and need looking after.

Here are some tips to make your gloves last a little bit longer.

DURABILITY TIPS

1. *Wash the palms of the gloves with warm water and soap when they are getting dirty. Let them dry naturally – don't put them on a radiator, as that will dry out the latex and make it more likely to crack.*

2. *Try to avoid pressing too hard on astroturf. If you are getting up after a dive, don't push up with your palms. Instead, use a closed fist.*

3. *Take off your gloves carefully after a game or training session; don't just yank them off!*

4. *Put the gloves next to or on top of each other when you're not playing, but don't leave them with the palms touching each other – latex can rip against itself.*

GLOVE STORY

Fingers: The fingers are crucial to the glove as they can improve grip, allow the hands to move naturally and, most importantly, provide protection against injury. A layer of foam, and in some cases a finger spine, can protect against fingers bending back. Ouch!

Palm: This is an important area of the glove for making those W catches (see page 59). Latex is the key material

here, but it can come in different forms: aqua latex gives
the gloves a stronger grip in wet conditions; thermal
lining can keep your hands warm in very cold weather;
or an extra-soft latex is useful for added grip on a muddy
pitch.

Strap: A velcro strap keeps the gloves tight and secure
on your wrists. But some goalkeepers prefer no strap
so it's smooth to slide on their hands, as it can feel less
restrictive. Whatever you choose, you need a glove that
will protect your wrist and that is securely fastened and
won't slip, no matter how wet the conditions.

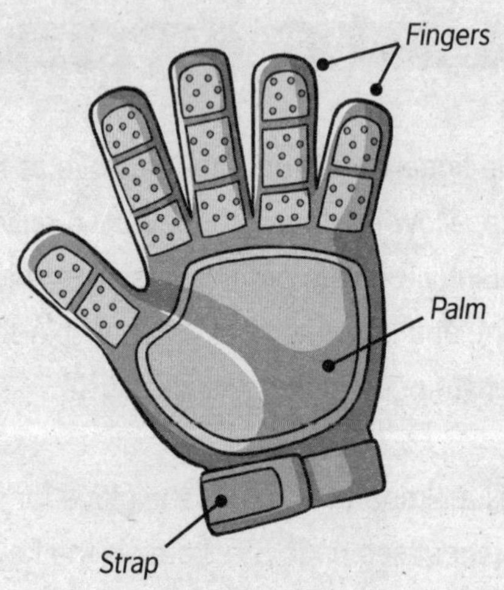

Backhand: The area on the back of the hand acts as a shield, absorbing powerful shots and protecting your bones. A lighter fabric and some air-mesh material will prevent sweaty hands. This is also where you can add a stylish logo or unique design to help the look. Italy goalkeeper Gigi Donnarumma had 288 spikes on his backhand at Euro 2020 to boost his punching power. Italy won the tournament, so it seemed to work!

Stitching: There are two options when it comes to the thread that holds the latex and the fabric together:
1. A rolled finger seam curves the latex around the fingertips. This gives a snug fit for goalkeepers who prefer to catch rather than block the ball.
2. A flat palm seam gives the latex palm a larger contact area. This is better for goalkeepers who prefer to block the ball, and is more likely to last longer.

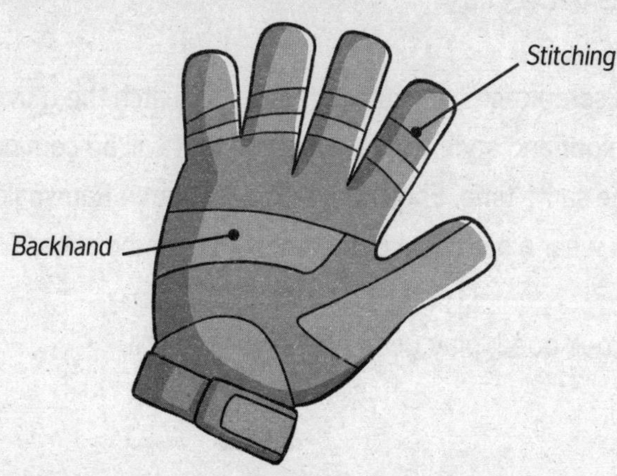

DESIGN SECRETS

Do you know what you will be wearing in three years' time? Probably not! Trends will have changed – the mullet fade that you once thought looked so cool might be out of fashion, and something else will be in!

Goalkeepers have to think this far into the future, as their gloves tend to be designed around three years before they hit the shops. It's a long process, as manufacturers will look at different colours, materials, straps and backhands to make the ideal glove.

Premier League goalkeepers work closely with glove-makers to get exactly what they want and need, including the precise finger width, finger length and wrist size for the perfect fit.

In some cases, manufacturers try to match the glove's colour and style with a new boot that will be coming out at the same time. England goalkeeper Aaron Ramsdale likes to wear a matching glove-and-boot combination.

'Look good, play good,' he says.

Ramsdale gets through around fifty pairs of gloves per season! (I do not recommend asking your parents for that many gloves!)

GLOVE DESIGN DRILL

1. Trace the outline of your hand on a blank piece of paper.

2. Design your own goalkeeper glove, using any colours and patterns you like.

Did you know? Goalkeeper glove manufacturers have only recently started making gloves specifically for female players. On average, female players have a longer thumb, a shorter little finger, and narrower fingers, palms and wrists than male players. Former England goalkeeper Carly Telford helped design female-friendly goalkeeper gloves, which are more comfortable for players with smaller hands. Every goalkeeper needs gloves that fit them properly!

GLOVE OF
MY LIFE

The score was 5–5 in the penalty shoot-out between
England and Portugal in the Euro 2004 quarter-final.
Portugal goalkeeper Ricardo saw England striker Darius
Vassell step up to take the next penalty. He panicked
because he had never seen Vassell take one before. He
had no idea what he would do!

Ricardo felt he needed to try something. So he looked
at his hands, he ripped off his gloves, and he threw them
behind the goal.* He raised his bare hands to Vassell, as
if to say, 'I don't even need gloves to save your penalty!'
It was a risky move.

Vassell looked at the referee to check that this was
allowed. It was. Suddenly, Vassell looked really nervous.
He took the shot. Ricardo dived the right way. He saved
the penalty!

Portugal needed to score the next penalty to win.
Ricardo was full of confidence after his save. He stepped

up to take the penalty himself. And guess what . . . he scored! No gloves, no problem!

Seven years after this game, Ricardo signed for Leicester City, whose main striker at the time was Vassell. On his first day at the club, their teammates made Vassell take another penalty against Ricardo to see if he could score the second time around. He took the penalty. Ricardo dived. And (this time with gloves on) he saved it again!

*Please note: do not take off your gloves before a penalty like Ricardo. You could end up with a nasty injury if you do!

QUICK CHANGE!

How quick are you at getting ready to play football?
Are you a slowcoach who spends hours looking for
their kit before eventually finding it (usually in the
exact place you left it)? Or are you a speedster, so
keen to get out there that you waste as little time
as possible in getting your kit on?

No way will you be as quick as England
goalkeeper Dean Henderson. He holds the world
record for 'fastest time to dress as a goalkeeper'.
In 2019, he earned his place in the history books
by putting on his socks, shorts, shirt, shin-pads,
boots and gloves in 49.51 seconds.

This Dean is keen!

Do you think you could be quicker than him?
Next time you're getting ready for a match, time
yourself to see if you can beat his record!

One of the most bizarre outfits worn by a goalkeeper was in 1907. Bradford City goalkeeper William Foulke turned up to a match wearing the same colour jersey as his opponents, Accrington Stanley. Englishman Foulke was over six foot tall and weighed more than twenty-three stone – at the time, given the average height was six inches shorter, that made him a giant!

He still holds the world record as the heaviest ever professional footballer. He weighed about the same as an adult panda – and about twice the average weight of a current Premier League footballer! And because of this, no one could find a replacement jersey big enough to fit him. So instead, it has been said that he wore a bedsheet tied around his body! Somehow, despite the unique outfit, Foulke managed not to concede any goals. This was one impressive clean sheet!

Foulke was a legendary figure in goalkeeping. His size intimidated opponents so much that one striker complained it was impossible to score a penalty against him because his body was blocking most of the goal. He was also a big character who had a bit of a temper. His outbursts were the stuff of legend. So legendary, in fact, that we cannot be totally sure that the stories told about him today are true. For example . . .

Foulke fell on top of an opponent and thought he'd squashed him to death (he hadn't!).

TRUE or FALSE

Foulke chased a referee into the dressing room, and the ref was so scared he hid in a cupboard.

TRUE or FALSE

Foulke punched the crossbar during a game and snapped it.

TRUE or FALSE

Foulke ate all of his Chelsea teammates' breakfasts, including his own, in one sitting.

TRUE or FALSE

Foulke invented ball boys, who were placed behind his goal to show off how big he was in comparison.

TRUE or FALSE

These stories helped define what fans thought a
goalkeeper should be: dominant and dramatic.
Always bringing main-character energy!

Here are a few things that we know to be true
about Foulke:

- He won the top division league title with Sheffield
  United in 1898.
- He won the FA Cup in 1899 and 1902.
- He played once for England, in a 4–0 win over
  Wales in 1897.
- Foulke was a brilliant goalkeeper.

Did you know? When a goalkeeper doesn't concede any goals in a game, they are said to have kept 'a clean sheet'. The name doesn't come from when Foulke wore the bedsheet (although some people think it does), but instead from when sports reporters used to record match results on white sheets of paper. If the 'goals conceded' column was blank at the end of the match, that meant no goals had been scored against the goalkeeper. A clean sheet!

SURF AND TURF

While we're on the subject of goalkeeper jerseys, you
need to meet Mexican player Jorge Campos. He is
one of the most unique goalkeepers in football history.
Campos was a surfer, a goalkeeper, a striker and a fashion
designer – and, on some occasions, all at the same time!

Campos actually designed his own goalkeeper jerseys,
which were inspired by his childhood spent surfing in
Acapulco, a city in Mexico famous for its golden beach,
bright green palm trees and glorious deep-blue seas.
To honour this time in his life, he created colourful
goalkeeper tops, often inspired by ancient Aztec patterns,
which made him stand out on the pitch.

Neon yellow – vibrant!
Bright green – eye-catching!
Blazing pink – flamboyant!

Campos's jerseys were a true reflection of himself and his
unique style.

His surfing background helped him as a goalkeeper. To be
a good surfer, you need core strength and fast reactions.
You need bravery and superb balance. And you need
great vision to look out for sharks!

You need similar skills to be a top goalkeeper – apart from
the shark-spotting!

When Campos was first signed by Mexican side Pumas
UNAM, he started out as a substitute goalkeeper. But in
training, he sometimes played as a striker, and he scored
lots of goals! So he asked the coach if he could play out of
goal instead. And in his second season, he got his chance.

It was the 1989–90 season, and Campos, who was
fast, skilful and courageous, ended up scoring fourteen

goals as a striker for Pumas. Amazing, right? But not as incredible as what happened next.

The following season, Campos was a starter in the team. This time, he was back in goal. He played an aggressive style, often catching the ball and then dribbling upfield himself. Sometimes, he would play a one-two (when you pass to a teammate who then passes the ball back to you) to get the ball into the opposition half or even into the opposition area!

At times, even though he was a goalkeeper, he was effectively playing as an attacking player! It was unusual, but the tactic was successful. With Campos in goal, Pumas won the Mexican league title in 1991.

By the time he moved to another club, Atlante, his double life as a goalkeeper-striker was well known. In one famous game in 1996 against Cruz Azul, Campos started in goal, made a bunch of great saves, but conceded one goal in the second half. The coach decided to make a substitution: he took off a striker, brought on a substitute goalkeeper and told Campos to play up front! With five minutes left, Campos volleyed an incredible equalizer into the far corner of the net to make it 1–1.

Campos said his experience of playing in attack helped him understand his opponents more when he was in goal. He knew that strikers try to trick the goalkeeper into thinking they will shoot in one direction, then aim for another. So he would often move slightly to one side of the goal first to get them to shoot where he wanted. This secret knowledge helped him save lots of shots!

Campos also turned the shirt-numbering system on its head. When he played in goal for Mexico at the 1996 Olympic Games, he wore the number nine shirt. In a match against Chile, despite starting in goal and wearing the number one shirt, he moved up front later in the game, still wearing the same shirt. And in that famous match against Cruz Azul? After the goalkeeper came on, he grabbed an outfield jersey that combined the positions of goalkeeper and centre forward, and wore the shirt number . . . nineteen!

Campos won many titles throughout his career, including the Mexican league and North American version of the Champions League; the MLS (Major League Soccer) Cup, the most prestigious trophy in the US and Canada; and twice the Gold Cup, which is North America's version of the Euros.

Campos remains one of Mexico's greatest ever players. His unique fashion sense reflected his dramatic style of play – both of which made him a true pioneer of goalkeeping. His kit designs even inspired goalkeepers of the future!

SHIRT DESIGN DRILL

1. Draw the shape of a T-shirt on a blank piece of paper.

2. Design your own goalkeeper shirt, using any colours and patterns you like. The brighter, the better!

COLOUR ME THIS

Before Campos burst on to the scene, goalkeepers mostly wore green jerseys. They rarely stood out. But the bright jerseys that Campos inspired might actually help with performance.

A group of scientists investigated the best colour top for goalkeepers to wear during a penalty shoot-out. They found that goalkeepers were most successful when wearing a red top. Red is often a colour associated with danger – and that might put strikers off!

Other goalkeepers believe that any bright colours will distract a striker and give them a tiny advantage. The eyes cannot ignore a bright colour, even if they want to, and therefore you become more likely to shoot towards the bright target that you see – and straight into the keeper's arms! That's why we see more and more goalkeepers wearing brightly coloured tops now.

ROGÉRIO CEM

Campos was not the only goalkeeper who scored goals and changed his shirt number as a result.

Brazilian goalkeeper Rogério Ceni was so bad at kicking when he started his career at São Paulo, one of Brazil's biggest teams, that defenders would take his goal kicks for him. But before training every day, he would practise his kicking. And slowly but surely, he started to improve.

As part of his practice, he tried to hit the crossbar from various positions on the pitch: often, he managed it! To master kicking with power and accuracy, he also hit a hundred free kicks every day. After years of this intense practice, it was clear that he had become the best free-kick taker in the São Paulo squad.

And so it proved: in 1997, four years after making his debut in the team, Ceni scored his first ever goal, a curling free kick in a 2–0 win. He continued to take free kicks for the team and scored the occasional penalty as well. In 2005, he became the team's official penalty-taker.

São Paulo had the most successful season in their history, winning the Brazilian league, the Copa Libertadores (the South American equivalent of the Champions League) and the Club World Cup. Their top scorer that season? Rogério Ceni! He scored twenty-one goals – ten penalties and eleven free kicks.

In 2007, Ceni changed his shirt number from one to zero-one. The reason? São Paulo did not have a number ten in the squad that season, so Ceni decided to reverse the number ten and make it zero-one. He saved like a number one and scored like a number ten!

Ceni remains a club legend at São Paulo. In 2011, he scored his hundredth goal, a record amount for a goalkeeper. He was nicknamed Rogério Cem (*cem* is one hundred in Portuguese, the language spoken in Brazil). When he retired in 2015, Ceni's goals total stood at 131.

São Paulo have retired the zero-one shirt in his honour, so no other São Paulo player will ever wear that number again – although goalkeepers at the club can still wear the number one shirt.

What we learned in this chapter

Jérémie Janot – Goalkeepers are superheroes.

Aaron Ramsdale – If you feel confident in what you're wearing, you will play better.

Carly Telford – Find gloves that are comfortable and fit properly.

Dean Henderson – You'll never be late if you can get changed quickly.

Jorge Campos – Balance, strength and bravery are important traits for goalkeepers (and surfers).

7

MINDSET

Bad news. There's a test at school today, and no one told you! You haven't revised, and you can't seem to remember anything you've learned this year.

The first question was hard. You probably got it wrong. That makes you worry a bit more about the next question. That one is even tougher, and you guess the answer. By the time question three comes along, your brain is scrambled.

Maybe you'll score a zero on this test! Your confidence is shattered. Broken. Destroyed.

It's OK, though, because at least you're reading the questions carefully and you're still focused . . . AAAHHH-TCHOOOO!!! What was that? Your teacher just did the biggest sneeze ever, and now you're trying not to laugh. You look up and catch your friend's eye. They cross their

eyes and stick out their tongue. Now you can't help
chuckling.

So you look down again and try to think of something to
stop the giggles. Grandma's chocolate cake. Ah yesssss,
delicious . . . ! The good news is you're no longer
laughing. But now you're thinking about how much you
want chocolate cake. That's not going to help in this test!

First, you lost your confidence. Now you've lost
your focus. You know you've already made some
mistakes. So how are you going to bounce back?
You're going to need some resilience.

Luckily, life as a goalkeeper can teach you exactly how
to develop all these traits.

Confidence is the belief in yourself and your abilities.
For a goalkeeper, confidence can make all the difference.
When you are confident, you are calmer, more motivated
and more focused. So when you feel like nothing will get
past you, you are actually more likely to catch every ball,
block every shot, make every pass. It's almost like the
game has slowed **. . . down . . . and . . . you . . . see . . .
everything . . . very . . . clearly!** This confident feeling

passes to your teammates who now trust in you, and will play better themselves as a result.

When a goalkeeper lacks confidence and is filled with self-doubt, this can lead to slower reactions, mistimed dives and misplaced kicks. This can make your teammates stressed and nervous, too, and means they will make mistakes as well. So a lack of confidence can create chaos in the whole squad!

Focus is the ability to concentrate with your full attention on something without getting distracted. It's a hard skill to master, and extremely important for goalkeepers, who can spend a lot of time not having much to do if lots of the action is in the opposition half. Hello? Are you still listening? I said that focus is important for goalkeepers!

Resilience is the ability to respond to different situations in the best way possible. For goalkeepers, this usually means recovering quickly from tough times on the pitch, like bouncing back after letting in a goal or making a mistake. (It can also mean adjusting to great times, like maintaining your focus after saving a penalty or winning a World Cup.) We can't avoid problems and setbacks, but for goalkeepers, whose mistakes can be costly, being resilient to them is a very important skill.

Goalkeepers have a more mentally challenging job than any other position. In this chapter, you will learn how to develop confidence, focus and resilience in order to make you a better goalkeeper. We will also meet the most patient goalkeeper in the world, one of the coolest goalkeepers in the world and the goalkeeper who proved medical experts wrong.

But first, we're going to meet the Dane who never stopped believing.

CONFIDENCE

Kasper Schmeichel was a young goalkeeper from Denmark with big dreams. After playing a handful of matches for Manchester City, he moved to a few different clubs across the lower divisions: Darlington, Bury, Falkirk, Notts County, as well as Cardiff City and Leeds United in the Championship.

Although people doubted whether he could play at the highest level, he never stopped believing in himself. He trusted in his abilities. He knew what his strengths were, he was open to feedback and he worked to improve his weaknesses. Above all, Schmeichel remained CONFIDENT.

One day, his old school asked him to visit and give a talk in assembly about being a goalkeeper. Schmeichel ended his talk with a line that summed up his confidence. He showed a photo of himself aged seven, standing next to the Premier League trophy. It was almost the same size as him! (He was able to get a photo beside the trophy because his dad, Peter, played for Manchester United and won the Premier League five times.)

'The next time I come back here, I will have won this trophy myself,' he said.

At the time, he was playing for Leicester City, who were not even in the Premier League. They were in the division below that, the Championship. However, they ended the season at the top of the Championship and so were promoted to the Premier League in 2014.

The task for most newly promoted teams is mainly to avoid relegation, which is when your team finishes in the bottom three positions and drops down to the division below. Leicester were bottom of the table for most of the season, but things turned around in their last few games, where they won seven of their last nine matches and just avoided relegation.

The next season began in 2015, and everyone expected them to be relegated. They started the season well and at the halfway stage were second in the league. Amazingly, it looked like they would avoid relegation again! They continued their good form in the second half of the season and, surprisingly, they went top of the table with fifteen games left to go.

That's still a lot of matches left to play, and bigger teams like Manchester City, Arsenal and Tottenham Hotspur were close behind them. But Leicester just kept on winning and remained top of the league for the rest of the season. No one could catch them!

Leicester winning the Premier League remains one of the biggest surprises in the history of English football. And while many people doubted whether they could do it, Schmeichel never stopped believing in his dream. After all, if he didn't believe it, who else would? This inner belief he had in himself is true confidence.

Confidence, for goalkeepers, is key to mastering communication, body language, positioning, distribution and shot-stopping. Being confident doesn't mean you are perfect or can stop everything, but that self-belief will help you perform your best on the pitch, and will then pass through to the rest of the team. If you believe it, you can be it! It worked for Schmeichel – and it can work for you too!

CON TRICK

Here's an exercise to improve your confidence. Close your eyes. (Actually, it might be quite hard to read with your eyes shut, so keep them open for now!)

When you've finished reading this section, close your eyes again. While they are closed, I want you to imagine this scene. You're in goal. You're wearing a cool jersey and nice gloves. You're playing in a cup final. And you're commanding your penalty area.

Picture this:

YOU telling your defenders where to stand before a set
piece.
YOU making a great save.
YOU passing the ball out smartly to teammates.
YOU using your positioning to prevent shots on goal.
YOU making another great save.
YOU being lifted on your teammates' shoulders after
victory!

Closing your eyes and imagining these scenarios is called visualization. Many players use visualization techniques as part of their pre-match routines to help their performance. It can calm nerves and improve decision-making and confidence. The reason is, if you picture yourself doing something well enough times, like saving a goal, your brain starts to believe it's possible! It can work before anything – whether that's a football match or a test at school.

CONFIDENCE DRILL

1. **Grab a piece of paper and a pencil.**

2. **Write down three moments you were proud of yourself and helped your team.**

3. **Next time you doubt yourself, look back over your list and remember how brilliant you are!**

FOCUS

It's a beautiful day. The sun is out, and it's not too hot. The smell of freshly mown grass is in the air. You can see people in the distance running around and having fun. It reminds you of the summer holidays when you muck around in the park, laughing with friends, having an ice cream . . . Now you really fancy an ice cream . . . Maybe you'll get one later, but what flavour? Now there's a good question. So many to choose from . . .

Wait a minute!

Someone's running towards you with a ball at their feet. People are shouting your name. What is going on?!

There you were, just enjoying a lovely daydream, and, suddenly, you remember. You're the goalkeeper and the opposition are coming towards your goal! You switched off for one second – or maybe three, or ten – and now you're under pressure. You need to focus!

This happens to goalkeepers quite a lot. Unlike in other positions, goalkeepers can face long periods of downtime during matches. One international goalkeeper used to make a shopping list in his head when things were quiet.

Spain goalkeeper Cata Coll believes the toughest part of being a goalkeeper is maintaining focus during these times.

'The hardest days are the matches where I'm standing still for most of it,' she says.

Her team is very good at keeping possession of the ball. Sometimes she will only touch the ball three times in a match! But even if the opponent only has one chance, she needs to be ready to stop it.

'You just have to learn ways to stay focused on the match in those moments.'

Keeping focus means you're always prepared for your next action as a goalkeeper. Without it, you could end up with poor positioning, slower reaction times, wasteful distribution and less communication with your defence – all of which could lead to conceding a goal. So how do Coll and other keepers keep their head in the game?

Here are some tips to help you stay focused during a match – and stop thinking of ice-cream flavours!

FOCUS TIPS

1. **Keep moving.** Small movements such as hopping from foot to foot, sidestepping or jogging on the spot can prevent stiffness and keep your mind alert and your body ready to react at any moment.

2. **Go through your checklist.** Create a list of things to check on during the game, such as the positions of your opponents and defenders, where the ball is and your own positioning too. Tracking the ball and adjusting your position as you go through your checks will keep you engaged in what's happening on the pitch.

3. **Keep talking.** Check in with your teammates, making sure they're focused and in the right positions too. Communicate clearly and positively. If they are too far away, you can always talk to yourself – this can build

**confidence, reduce stress and keep you
ready to go. You can use phrases like:**

- **I'm ready for this!**
- **I'm in the right position – bring it on!**
- **I'm calm, strong and fast – let's go!**
- **Eyes on the ball!**
- **Stay sharp!**
- **This is the moment!**

Did you know? Young Danish goalkeeper Niels Bohr was distracted when he was in goal for his local team, Akademisk Boldklub, in the early 1910s. The story goes that he conceded eighteen goals in the first half – apparently, he didn't even notice when one went in! After the game, he claimed it was because he was solving a mathematical puzzle in his head that was bothering him. Maybe it was worth it. Bohr went on to win a Nobel Prize in Physics for his groundbreaking work investigating atoms. He wasn't the best goalkeeper of all time, but he was definitely one of the smartest!

FOCUS ON HANNAH

There's another definition of focus that is important for goalkeepers. This kind of focus is all about how clearly your eyes can see something.

Before I tell this next story, I want to let you know that you don't need to worry if your vision is not perfect. Many goalkeepers wear contact lenses to improve their eyesight. And although one goalkeeper was once told that her eyesight would make it impossible for her to even play sports at all, she now plays football for England!

Hannah Hampton was born with an eye misalignment, which is when one eye is turned in a slightly different direction to the other eye. It means she finds it difficult to judge distances and how near or far away something is.

Hampton had three operations on her eyes before she turned five. None were totally successful, but she didn't let it stop her playing, and loving, football.

She moved to Spain aged five and played as a striker for a team called Villarreal. She was fast and could strike the ball just as well with either foot. She then moved back to England and played in Stoke City's academy aged ten. In her very first match, the goalkeeper was injured in the warm-up, and Hampton stepped in. She played brilliantly! It just so happened that an England scout was watching the game and was very impressed by Hampton. Aged just twelve, she was invited to an England under-15 camp to train as a goalkeeper with the squad. She did so well that she was invited back again and again. She began playing for England youth teams and eventually made her full England debut aged twenty-two.

Judging distances is very important for goalkeepers, so it is extraordinary that Hampton achieved her goal of playing for England. One eye expert believes that Hampton's brain has been able to adapt and realize that the vision from the misaligned eye is not reliable, and therefore learned to ignore it. But it hasn't always been easy for her. When she was younger, she once put her hands in the wrong place to catch the ball and broke her finger. On another occasion, the ball hit her in the face, and she got a nosebleed.

'Me being a goalkeeper shouldn't really work in theory,' she said. 'But it just does!'

You can say that again! Hampton's performances helped England reach (and ultimately win) the Euro 2025 final. She set up a goal with an astonishing long pass in a victory over the Netherlands. And, after another nosebleed when she was struck by a stray elbow, she went on to save two penalties in a dramatic shoot-out against Sweden, with tissue stuck up one nostril!

The final against Spain also went to a penalty shoot-out. Hampton saved two penalties, and another missed the target, to help England to a historic success. It was the first time an England team had ever won a major tournament played outside of England.

'When people say you can't do things, you absolutely can do them if you believe in yourself and really want to give things a go,' she says. 'Hopefully, my journey can prove to others that you can do whatever you set your mind to. I'll never stop telling people to follow their dreams.'

Hampton has mastered her focus in both senses of the word – which makes her a truly talented goalkeeper.

RESILIENCE

Iceland's Hannes Halldórsson had been waiting for this moment for fourteen years. It was his first time starting for his local side, a third-division team in Iceland called Leiknir. And it was a huge game: the last match of the season, against rivals Víkingur Ólafsvík, with the winners earning promotion to the second division. It was the biggest match in the history of Leiknir.

Halldórsson was only playing because Valur Gunnarsson, the first-choice goalkeeper, had been sent off in the previous game and was suspended. Halldórsson was desperate to make a name for himself. He invited television news crews to cover the game in the hope that his performance would attract some attention. And it did – just not in the way he dreamed.

Leiknir were 1–0 down when Halldórsson took a goal kick. But instead of kicking the ball, he accidentally kicked the ground (maybe he hadn't practised the kicking drills on page 114). The ball rolled a few yards forward, straight to a Víkingur striker, who passed to a teammate to score, sealing Víkingur's win and promotion. The game was covered on the national news that night, with the headline 'Goalkeeper's Horrible Mistake.'

Halldórsson was heartbroken. He went to his parents' house, sat in their basement and listened to music with the lights turned off. For the next few years, all anyone talked about was 'the Hannes kick', as his mistake became known. He thought a lot about quitting football entirely, but he decided that he wanted to make up for the error and prove himself.

He joined another club in the third division, and every day he practised his goal kicks for an hour so he would never make the same mistake again. He played really well, and after a couple of years, earned a move to a new club in the top division.

Within a few more years, Halldórsson was selected for the Iceland national team. What an honour! Iceland is a tiny country, but became the smallest nation (by population) to qualify for a major tournament when they reached Euro 2016. Halldórsson was a key part of their success: they reached the quarter-final and knocked out England along the way.

Two years later, Iceland were in the 2018 World Cup. Halldórsson started their first game against Argentina. With the score at 1–1, Argentina won a penalty. Up stepped Lionel Messi, one of the world's greatest players, against Halldórsson, the goalkeeper whose horrible mistake had once made the national news. And as if the pressure wasn't enough, there were millions of people watching all over the world.

Halldórsson had already thought about what he would do in this situation. He knew he wanted to dive to his right. He didn't change his mind. Messi kicked the ball. The goalkeeper dived the right way . . . and he saved the penalty!

By responding to that big mistake in his first game with resilience, Halldórsson was able to achieve his dream. Rather than quitting football and letting the mistake define him, he picked himself back up, laced up his boots, stuck on his gloves and kept going. And that is what resilience is all about!

Showing resilience still allows you to be upset if something goes wrong. In fact, it's very important to sit with those feelings. But it also means not giving up, then keeping your cool, trying again and, most importantly, learning from the experience. Halldórsson chose not to give up and turn his back on football – and he ended up saving a World Cup penalty against Lionel Messi!

Gunnarsson, the goalkeeper who was suspended for that crucial game for Leiknir, believes that Halldórsson's mistake actually helped him become a better goalkeeper. It allowed Halldórsson to learn and improve – and he never made that same mistake again!

RESILIENCE FROM THE BENCH

There's one position that requires even more resilience than the goalkeeper.

This person has trained as hard as they can all week. They wear the team kit. They've listened to all the team talks. And yet . . . they might not be called into action for the whole game. Or the next game. Or the one after that!

Welcome to the strange world of the substitute goalkeeper.

There tend to be two different types of substitute goalkeeper.

1. A player who definitely knows they are the reserve goalkeeper. They may be young and waiting for an opportunity, or experienced and coming to the end of their career.

2. A player who believes they should be the number one and wants to challenge the current goalkeeper.

Most coaches prefer picking option one as their substitute goalie, as it can be disruptive to a team environment if both goalkeepers are demanding to play. Of course, only one of them can play, and so coaches try to avoid feelings of disappointment and negativity from the other.

The ideal substitute is the player who accepts their place in the team and is prepared to work hard and push the number one to be better. They can do this by playing their best in training, even though they know they're

unlikely to play anytime soon; cheering on the number one and being supportive during games; and sharing advice and tips when they can.

The perfect example of a substitute goalkeeper is Englishman Steve Harper. He signed for Newcastle in 1993 when he was eighteen years old. He waited five years to make his first appearance. He was the reserve goalkeeper for eighteen seasons out of twenty at Newcastle, and in ten of those seasons, he didn't make a single league appearance.

Despite this, Harper continued to work hard in training. And while he always supported the first-choice goalkeeper, he once revealed that he did sometimes struggle and doubt himself. He even asked his coaches if he could play more games. But when they kept him on the bench, he never complained. He just kept on working hard. This was his way of showing resilience.

His twenty years as a Newcastle player is longer than anyone has ever been at the club. And though he's now retired as a goalkeeper, he still works there as head of the youth academy, looking after the next generation of talent. Resilience wins!

WE ALL MAKE MISTAKES

Football is full of goalkeepers who have made mistakes. If it can happen to top professional players, it may happen to you. So while it can feel very embarrassing at the time, just remember we've all been there! Here are some of the most embarrassing goalkeeper moments in football history – hopefully these will remind you that whatever you did, it probably wasn't as bad as you think.

Shay Given (Newcastle)

What happened: Given caught the ball and then rolled it forward so he could take a long kick upfield. He had not spotted that Coventry forward Dion Dublin was lurking behind him, who nipped ahead of Given and kicked the ball into the empty net.

What they said: Commentators joked that Given was the only Irishman who did not know where Dublin was!

Embarrassment rating: 😳 😳 😳

Peter Enckelman (Aston Villa)

What happened: In a derby match against rivals Birmingham City, Villa player Olof Mellberg took a throw-in to Enkelman. The ball rolled under his foot and into the goal, clipping his studs as it went past him. As he had made contact with the ball, the referee had no option but to award a goal.

What he said: 'It should have been the easiest thing in the world to control, but I missed it and the next thing I knew, it was in the net. Sorry for my mistake.'

Embarrassment rating: 😳 😳 😳 😳

Alexander Sollner (Grunbach)

What happened: On a very windy day, Sollner had a goal kick, which he let midfielder Oliver Wiedemann take. Wiedemann hit the ball high, but a huge gust of wind pushed it back towards goal, where it landed in the area. It bounced over Sollner's head and into the net for one of the strangest own goals in history.

What should have happened: The rules state that you cannot score an own goal directly from a goal kick – and as no other player touched the ball, the referee should have awarded a corner.

Embarrassment rating:    

Did you know? Brazil hosted the 1950 World Cup and were huge favourites to win the final against Uruguay. Nearly 200,000 Brazil fans came to watch the game at the Maracanã stadium, as they wanted to see their team win its first World Cup. It remains a world record for the biggest crowd ever at a game.

Unfortunately for them, with eleven minutes to go, Brazil goalkeeper Moacir Barbosa conceded a goal, and Brazil lost 2–1. Barbosa was blamed for the defeat and was never allowed to visit the Brazil team again for fear he would bring them bad luck. He ended up working at the Maracanã, and every day he looked out on to the pitch where he made the mistake that cost his country their first World Cup win. Eventually, he was given the wooden goalposts from the stadium as a memento.

He invited his friends around for a meal. He lit a barbecue and burnt the goalposts that had caused him, and the country he loved, so much sadness. Then he cooked a thick steak with onion and vinegar sauce and ate it with a smile on his face. Delicious!

RESILIENCE TIPS

During the game:

- *Remember, it's impossible to be perfect and even the best goalkeepers make mistakes.*
- *If you do make an error, focus on the present moment and your next save.*
- *Next time you catch a cross or make a save, be positive and congratulate yourself.*
- *Use positive body language and keep communicating with your teammates so they know you're focused and your head's in the game.*

After the game:

- *Wait until you're ready, and then you can analyse your performance.*
- *Think about where you might have gone wrong and what you could do better next time.*
- *Work on those aspects so you don't repeat the mistake!*

DANGEROUS JOB

This story comes with a health warning. Do not try this at home! Or on the football pitch!

It happened in the 1956 FA Cup final, which was played between Manchester City and Birmingham City.

With fifteen minutes to go, Manchester City goalkeeper Bert Trautmann rushed out to catch a cross. He collided at speed with Birmingham striker Peter Murphy, whose leg smashed into his neck. Trautmann was knocked unconscious. He came round soon after, but his vision was blurred, he was feeling dizzy, and he could not move his neck. There were no substitutes in those days. His City teammates told him to go off, but he wanted to stay on. Incredibly, and dangerously, he played on.

Despite being in agony and holding his neck up with his right hand, Trautmann made two more saves, and Manchester City somehow ended up winning 3–1. Trautmann later found out he had continued playing with a broken bone in his neck, and was extremely lucky not to have made the injury worse.

Thankfully, this would never happen today. If you have any kind of injury on the football pitch, you must tell a responsible adult and stop playing immediately. It's never sensible to play on with an injury.

What we learned in this chapter

Kasper Schmeichel – Believe in yourself.

Cata Coll – Keep your focus at all times, even when the ball is in the opposition half.

Hannah Hampton – With focus, hard work and determination, you can do whatever you set your mind to.

Hannes Halldórsson – Learn from your mistakes so you don't repeat them.

Moacir Barbosa – Barbecues are nicer if you don't cook with goalposts.

Bert Trautmann – Do NOT play on if you are injured.

8 SUPERSTITIONS

Meet Stefan Frei. He's a Swiss goalkeeper who has played more than 300 times for the American MLS team Seattle Sounders. This is his pre-match routine:

1. Jump into the dressing-room hot tub before any teammates arrive.
2. Tape up each finger to protect them from injury.
3. Throw any extra tape in the bin. (If he misses the bin, he starts the taping process from the beginning.)
4. Drink a beetroot juice.
5. Lay out three pieces of chewing-gum: one for the warm-up and one for each half of the match.
6. Eat a banana.
7. Pop in chewing-gum piece number one.
8. Go on to the pitch for stretches and warm-up drills, always in the same order.
9. Put on the right shin-pad before the left one.

10. Recite a prayer with one hand on the jersey crest
    on his shirt, before putting it on.
11. Remind himself that his dog (which died) will be
    watching.
12. Pop in chewing-gum piece number two.
13. Speak to the right goalpost (he usually says: 'Let's
    go together!'), then hit it low down using the palm
    of his hand.
14. Speak to the left goalpost, then hit it high up.
15. At kick-off, raise both arms up and take a deep
    breath.

Frei does not call himself superstitious, which means
believing that certain objects or actions can bring good
luck. He prefers to describe what he does before every
match as a routine. His routine gives him comfort which,
in turn, makes him feel more confident, prepared and
ready for the challenge ahead.

As he puts it: 'I've done so much, and there's no way
the opponent did the same amount.' You can say that
again, Stefan!

Lots of goalkeepers are known for having strange
superstitions and pre-match routines, involving all sorts

of bizarre things, including holy water, toasties, scissors
– and even kissing a teammate!

In this chapter, we'll examine some of these weird and
wonderful habits. We will meet the World Cup finalist
who had one particularly wee-ird routine. And, if you
want one, I'll help you come up with your very own
routine too!

Before we start, I should say that I don't really believe
that laying out gum in a certain position will make you
a better goalkeeper. And I'm not saying that thinking of
your dog will help you catch crosses, or that muttering
to the goalposts will improve your chances of saving a
penalty.

The truth is, the way to become the best goalkeeper you
can possibly be is to work on all the things we've talked
about in the book before this chapter – the positioning,
the diving, the catching, the passing, the communication
and most importantly of all, the mindset.

If you are committed to practising and improving, always
trying your best and being a supportive team player,
then I am sure you will be a fantastic goalkeeper!

But that doesn't mean we can't have some fun in this
final chapter, looking at the funny and odd superstitions
or routines that some goalkeepers have.

Are you wearing your lucky pants? You might need
them for this!

URINE GOAL!

Argentina reached the 1990 World Cup final thanks to their goalkeeper Sergio Goycochea, who helped them win TWO penalty shoot-outs. In doing so, he invented a rare and rather disgusting superstition that you need to know about. As long as you DO NOT TRY THIS YOURSELF!

The quarter-final was between Argentina and Yugoslavia, and it ended 0–0 after extra time. Goycochea had drunk a lot of water during the game, so before the penalty shoot-out, he was desperate for a wee! The rules then stated that no player was allowed to leave the pitch. So he told his teammates about his predicament, and they stood around him while he did what he needed to do. In other words, he did a wee . . . in his shorts. He was lucky the shorts were black, so there were no awkward stains!

Goycochea saved two penalties in that shoot-out, and Argentina moved to the semi-final against tournament hosts Italy.

That game ended 1–1 and, once again, it went to a penalty shoot-out. This time, Goycochea did not need a wee. But because things had gone so well for him last time, he decided to repeat – or wee-peat – exactly what he'd done before the previous shoot-out. So, once again, he asked his teammates to hide him, as he peed through his shorts. It was another successful shoot-out!

From that moment on, he did the same thing before every shoot-out he faced. He said it was his lucky charm. Even if there's nothing charming about it!

KISSES, SCISSORS . . . AND EVERYTHING ELSE

Fabien Barthez (France)

During the 1998 World Cup, France goalkeeper Fabien Barthez received a big kiss on the forehead before every match from his teammate Laurent Blanc. The players thought it brought the team luck, and it seemed to work! France only conceded two goals in their seven games, and they won the tournament for the first time in their history. Blanc, a defender, scored a dramatic winning goal in their Round of 16 win over Paraguay. Even though Blanc was suspended for the World Cup final after receiving a red card in the previous match, he donned his full kit and still kissed Barthez on the forehead before the match against Brazil. France won 3–0. (The two players both ended up playing together again for Manchester United in 2001. They did not continue the pre-match kissing, but it made no difference: United still won the Premier League in 2003!)

Iker Casillas (Spain)

Casillas was twenty years old when he was named as a Real Madrid substitute for the 2002 Champions League final. He was not expecting to play, and was not ready when first-choice goalkeeper César Sánchez went off injured in the second half. Casillas always felt more comfortable wearing short sleeves, but he had a long-sleeved shirt on when he was called up to play. As he was too nervous to play with long sleeves, the game was delayed while someone found small medical scissors and hacked off his long sleeves! Casillas felt so much better with the short sleeves, and he made a series of incredible saves to help Madrid win that Champions League final. Only ever wearing short sleeves, he went on to help Real Madrid win five league titles and three Champions Leagues; and with Spain, two Euros and, as captain, one World Cup. His short sleeves were a shortcut . . . to trophies!

Alan Rough (Scotland)

Rough had so many superstitions before and even during a match, it's amazing he had the time to make any saves at all! He played over fifty times for Scotland, so they must have helped him. He always took certain objects to matches – including an old tennis ball, a keyring with an image of a thistle, and a star-shaped medal. Underneath his jersey, he always wore a number eleven shirt, the same number he wore as a young boy.

He would always bounce the ball off the tunnel wall three times before going on to the pitch. And he would always kick the ball into an empty net when he approached his goal for the first time. During the match, he'd often ask the referee for the time. He would regularly blow his nose using a hankie that he tucked inside a cap. And he would always chew seven pieces of chewing-gum each game: three in each half and one for the last five minutes, when things got exciting! Rough used to worry about forgetting one of his routines. 'I don't think I could play without these preparations,' he once said.

A JUICY STORY

Fans often invent rituals of their own when it comes to supporting their team, and occasionally these rituals can affect the players. That was the case for Hull City's Scottish goalkeeper Ian McKechnie, who once bumped into two fans near the stadium on a quiet Thursday afternoon while he was eating an orange.

At Hull's next home game, two oranges were thrown into his net. Assuming they were from the fans he met, McKechnie ate them during quiet moments in the game.

That started a craze: at every home match, before kick-off and at half-time, fans threw oranges into McKechnie's net. One orange even had the words 'I LOVE YOU' written on it! During one half-time break, more than

600 oranges were thrown into his goal. The second half started late, as staff had to come and clear them all away.

McKechnie was a popular goalkeeper who also played for Arsenal and Southend United. He died in 2015, and can you guess what happened at his funeral? His friends and family all threw oranges into his grave.

MAKE YOUR OWN SUPERSTITION

Would you like to have your own superstition? If so, here are some suggestions – see if there's any that you'd like to try!

KIT

Left! Right! Right! Left! Do you always put your left sock on before your right sock? Or the other way around? Can you even remember?! Some goalkeepers will always put their left sock or boot or glove (or all of them) on before their right. Others have an item that they wear under their kit whenever they play.

Example: Brazil goalkeeper Ederson wore the same pair of boxer shorts for every game – for eight years! He did wash them in between, thankfully!

MEALS

A balanced meal combining carbohydrates (such as pasta), protein (for example, chicken or tofu) and

vegetables (carrots or broccoli, for instance)
is ideal before a match. Many players are
superstitious about what they eat and like to stick to
the same pre-match meal. What would you go for?
Remember, it has to be healthy!

Examples: Spain goalkeeper Pepe Reina always ate
a ham-and-cheese toastie the night before a game.
Australia goalkeeper Mackenzie Arnold prefers spaghetti
Bolognese the night before a match, and toast with
poached eggs and avocado on game day. Delicious!

THE GOAL

Some goalkeepers have rituals based around the goal,
whether that's the posts, crossbar, net or goal line.
Remember, you are protecting a precious part of the
pitch that no one else spends as much time with. Treat
that goal as your own, and look after it!

Examples: Russia goalkeeper Artyom Rebrov kissed
his goalposts and spoke to them before every game.
Belgium goalkeeper Thibaut Courtois always touches the
crossbar at the start of each half.

OBJECTS

Some goalkeepers carry a little kit bag that they keep in
their goal. Often it contains a drink, a cap and, for some
goalkeepers, an object that they believe brings them luck.
You could even sneak in this book! Just don't read it
during the match (even if it might be tempting)!

Example: Ireland goalkeeper Shay Given carried
a small vial of holy water in his kit bag. Many Roman
Catholics believe the water carries special powers.

NOTHING AT ALL

Or maybe, having read this book, you realize you don't
need any superstitions at all!

You've done your warm-ups. You've got all the right kit.
You're mentally focused and prepared. You know what
to do: get your positioning right, pass sensibly and keep
talking to your teammates. Use your strong mental attitude
to get you through tough parts of the game. Don't dwell on
any mistakes – take the opportunity to bounce back and
show your talent. By the end of the game, you could be
the hero for your team!

YOU'VE GOT THIS!

What we learned in this chapter

Stefan Frei – A routine can bring comfort and confidence.

Sergio Goycochea – There is **never** an excuse to wee on the pitch.

Ian McKechnie – Eating fruit is always a healthy option . . . but maybe not during the game!

Mackenzie Arnold – Make sure your pre-match meals are balanced and healthy.

Artyom Rebrov – Show some love for the goal you're protecting.

GLOSSARY

The language of goalkeeping can be confusing. After all, for goalkeepers, clean sheets have nothing to do with the laundry and a wall is not just on one side of a room. No wonder people say goalkeepers are different! The following terms will help you understand the role of the goalkeeper, and in some cases, what goalkeepers are talking about. So get your gloves off and let's dive in.

Agility – the ability to quickly change direction or speed. Goalkeepers need agility to dive in one direction and get up quickly in case another save needs to be made.

Anchor – the player on the outside of a defensive wall, closest to the near post, placed before a free kick. The anchor should not duck or turn their backs once the free kick has been struck, so it helps if the anchor is tall . . . and brave!

Assist – the last touch or pass from a player that leads to a teammate scoring a goal. Almost all goals come from an assist, whether it's from a corner, free kick or even a long kick from the goalkeeper. Brazilian goalkeeper Ederson is the goalkeeper with the most Premier League assists.

At full stretch – for goalkeepers, this is when they extend their bodies or arms as far as they can while trying to stop the ball. It can also refer to using as much effort as possible.

Backpass – a deliberate pass back to the goalkeeper, who is not allowed to pick up the ball with their hands. They must clear it with their feet, otherwise a free kick is awarded from where the ball was handled. The backpass rule was established in 1992 and caused many goalkeepers problems. This has encouraged all goalkeepers to practise skills with their feet!

Clean sheet – achieved when one team doesn't let in a goal during a game. So if your team wins 3–0, your goalkeeper (and the defenders) kept a clean sheet . . . although they might have got muddy knees!

Clean through – this refers to a player, usually a striker, who is running towards the goal with no defenders in the way, and only the goalkeeper to beat. Strikers are

expected to score when they are clean through, so it's
a great opportunity for the goalkeeper to become the
hero!

Cross – a pass from an area of the pitch near the
touchline towards the middle, usually near the
opposition goal. The goalkeeper's job is to catch or
block the cross before it gets to a striker – which might
make the striker cross!

Defensive actions – these refer to tackles, interceptions,
blocks, saves and catches made by players to stop the
opposition from scoring. These actions are not only
executed by defensive players – in some teams, strikers
do a lot of defending too – but the defenders and
goalkeeper are the skilled specialists in this area.

Drop-kick – when the goalkeeper drops the ball
from their hands and kicks it just as it hits the ground.
It's a way for goalkeepers to hit long passes to their
teammates further up the pitch.

Instep – the part of the foot that players often use to
kick the ball. It's the long area between your big toe and
your ankle, and kicking there helps with accuracy.

Knockout game – a match played in a tournament where defeat will end in elimination. These happen towards the end of tournaments like the World Cup and the Champions League. If a knockout match is tied at the end of the game, teams might play extra time, which is another thirty minutes, split into two fifteen-minute halves. If the scores are still level, then the game will go to a penalty shoot-out. That's when the goalkeeper can make all the difference!

Laws of the Game – the official title for the rules of football. They were first written in 1863 by the English Football Association. In 1866, the International Football Association Board, known as IFAB, took charge of the Laws of the Game and now, over 150 years later, are still responsible for establishing rules to keep the game safe and enjoyable for everyone.

Lob – a shot that goes in the air and over the head of the goalkeeper. A lob is usually struck when the ball is off the ground (for example, after a bounce). Not to be confused with a chip, which is a shot that goes over the goalkeeper's head, but is usually struck when the ball is on the ground.

Long ball – a pass that moves the ball a long distance
from one end of the pitch to another. It's normally
hit by a goalkeeper or defender in the air, aiming
for an attacking player. It's a way to move the ball
quickly up the pitch, but comes with the risk that an
opponent will win possession of the ball straight away.

Narrowing the angle – an important tactic for
goalkeepers to reduce the space between the goalkeeper
and the ball, therefore reducing the time and open space
available for the striker to aim at the goal. This move
puts strikers under pressure, and is a great opportunity
for goalkeepers to make decisive saves.

Near post – the post closest to the ball when a player
is shooting or crossing. The far post is the post furthest
away from the ball when a player is shooting or crossing.
Part of the goalkeeper's job is to make sure the area
between the goalkeeper and each post is equally
protected.

One-on-one – this is one of the trickiest moments for
a goalkeeper to face: when a player with the ball faces
just one opponent, usually the goalkeeper, with no other
defenders in the way. The goalkeeper needs to decide

whether to run towards the ball and the striker or wait. The decision depends on many factors, including how far away the ball is from goal and how good the striker might be!

One-two – when a player passes to a teammate, runs past a defender, and the teammate passes the ball back to them. One plus one equals two. But one pass plus another pass equals a one-two!

Outfield player – any player on the pitch that is not the goalkeeper.

Pass completion rate – the calculation of how many passes by a player reach their teammates. If a goalkeeper makes ten passes in a match and nine of them go straight to their teammate, the pass completion rate is 90 per cent. 

Pressing – a tactic that involves pressuring and tackling the opposition when they have the ball to cause them to make a mistake or lose possession. Goalkeepers are often 'pressed' in possession, as winning the ball close to the opposition goal can lead to a disorganized defence and a shot. Goalkeepers need to stay composed and pass well when opponents are pressing. A high press

is when this happens in the opposition's penalty area,
when winning possession can lead to a very quick shot.

Rebound – when the ball bounces off a post, opponent
or teammate after a shot on goal. Goalkeepers need to
be particularly alert to rebounds, as making one save
is not always enough. The ball might rebound to an
opponent for them to score. Try to avoid this!

Rising shot – a shot that causes the ball to rise into the
air, which can be hard for goalkeepers to stop. The shot
is struck from below the centre of the ball, and the skill
to keep the ball out of the goal requires a high leap, long
arm stretch and a strong hand.

Run-up – when a player takes a few steps before kicking
the ball. Players often use a run-up for free kicks, goal
kicks or penalty kicks to get more power and accuracy.
Some goalkeepers watch the angle of a player's run-up
before a penalty to work out where they might be aiming
the ball. The run-up could provide a clue!

Set piece – when the ball is returned into play after
it goes off the pitch, or after a foul. These include free
kicks, corners, throw-ins and penalties, and they lead to

around 30 per cent of all goals scored. Goalkeepers need to be organized and communicate with their team before a set piece, so all the defenders know their exact role before the ball is struck.

Substitutes' bench – the place where substitute players sit during the game. A substitute is a player not in the starting eleven but who can come on in the match to replace a player who might be tired or injured. (Up to five substitutes can play during a game, with one more allowed if the game goes to extra time.) Traditionally, substitutes sat on an actual bench (along with the coach) on one side of the pitch. Nowadays, most substitutes have their own individual seat from where they watch the game.

Unmarked – when a player does not have an opponent close to them. An unmarked player has more time to pass, shoot or score because they are not under pressure. If a goalkeeper spots an unmarked opponent near to goal, their job is to alert a teammate to the danger!

Visualization – when you close your eyes before a game (not right now – you need to read this!) and use your imagination to picture yourself playing well in a match. You might imagine yourself saving a penalty, catching a cross or making a save in a one-on-one. If you can imagine it happening, it can help you feel confident and ready, because your brain has shown you what it looks like!

Volley – when you kick the ball before it hits the ground. Goalkeepers will most often volley the ball when they have it in their hands by dropping it and kicking it before it touches the ground. Some goalkeepers like to side-volley the ball, which involves dropping the ball on one side and swinging their leg sideways, almost like a roundhouse karate kick. A side-volley goes fast and low and is often more accurate than a standard volley.

Wall – when players stand together in a line to block the ball and cover the goal during a free kick. The goalkeeper sets up the wall to their preference, choosing the number of players and exact positioning to ensure the wall is protecting as much of the goal as possible. The wall must stay together once the ball is struck, otherwise it might sneak between two players and end up in the goal.

ACKNOWLEDGEMENTS

Just as every goalkeeper needs help from their defence to be successful, so it was a team effort to get this book into your hands. Thanks to everyone at Puffin Books, especially Phoebe Jascourt, Fenella Bates, Melissa Mackey, Ben Hughes, Daisy Northway, Lauren Floodgate, Memoona Zahid, George Maudsley, Hollie Cayzer and Dynamo Limited.

Thanks to my agent Claire Conrad, and the team at Janklow & Nesbit: Kirsty Gordon, Olivia Everitt, Corina Brodersen and Will Francis.

A special shout-out to Hugo Oliveira, who kindly shared his extraordinary knowledge and has provided ideas, support and inspiration over many years; and to Hans Leitert, always available and curious – the original Safe Hans! These two goalkeeping wizards taught me just how much there is to say about this complicated craft. *Obrigado, amigos!*

I'm also grateful to my friends and colleagues who helped with research for this book. These include: Toby Aldous, Jon Arnold, Joachim Barbier, Adam Bate, Alex Bellos, Jeff Benjamin, Ryan Benson, John Brown, Mark Carey, George Caulkin, Petr Čech, Marcus Christenson, Tim Dittmer, Mark Duell, Ederson, Chris Evans, Ben Foster, Brian Glanville, John Goodby, Phil Hay, James Horncastle, Graham Hunter, Alex Ibaceta, Stuart James, Deborah Linton, Christophe Lollichon, Sid Lowe, Nick Miller, James Montague, Matt Pentz, Alexandre Plumey, Matt Pyzdrowski, Guillermo Rai, Art de Roché, David Segar, Dan Sheldon, Sarah Shephard, Darren Tulett, Lauren Ward, Dr Anthony White, Jonny Whitmore Jonathan Wilson and Ethan Zohn.

Thanks as always to Annie, Clemmy and Bibi, the dream defence for any goalkeeper, for their support, patience and checking that my jokes are still terrible. IYKYK!

IF YOU ENJOYED THIS, YOU'LL LOVE

SCORE LIKE A STRIKER

AVAILABLE NOW!